D1351375

A Place in the Country

A Place in the Country

W. G. SEBALD

On Gottfried Keller, Johann Peter Hebel,
Robert Walser and Others

Translated from the German and
with an introduction by Jo Catling

HAMISH HAMILTON
an imprint of
PENGUIN BOOKS

HAMISH HAMILTON

Published by the Penguin Group
Penguin Books Ltd, 80 Strand, London WC2R ORL, England
Penguin Group (USA) Inc., 375 Hudson Street, New York, New York 10014, USA
Penguin Group (Canada), 90 Eglinton Avenue East, Suite 700, Toronto, Ontario, Canada M4P 2Y3
(a division of Pearson Penguin Canada Inc.)
Penguin Ireland, 25 St Stephen's Green, Dublin 2, Ireland (a division of Penguin Books Ltd)
Penguin Group (Australia), 707 Collins Street, Melbourne, Victoria 3008, Australia
(a division of Pearson Australia Group Pty Ltd)
Penguin Books India Pvt Ltd, 11 Community Centre, Panchsheel Park, New Delhi – 110 017, India
Penguin Group (NZ), 67 Apollo Drive, Rosedale, Auckland 0632, New Zealand
(a division of Pearson New Zealand Ltd)
Penguin Books (South Africa) (Pty) Ltd, Block D, Rosebank Office Park, 181 Jan Smuts Avenue,
Parktown North, Gauteng 2193, South Africa

Penguin Books Ltd, Registered Offices: 80 Strand, London WC2R ORL, England

www.penguin.com

First published in German as *Logis in einem Landhaus* 1998

This translation first published 2013
001

Copyright © The Estate of W. G. Sebald, 2013
Translation, introduction and notes copyright © Jo Catling, 2013

The moral right of the author and translator has been asserted

Photographs of Robert Walser used with grateful acknowledgement to KEYSTONE.

Set in Perpetua Std 12.75 / 16 pt
Typeset by Palimpsest Book Production Limited, Falkirk, Stirlingshire
Printed in Great Britain by Clays Ltd, St Ives plc

A CIP catalogue record for this book is available from the British Library

ISBN: 978-0-241-14418-3

www.greenpenguin.co.uk

MIX
Paper from
responsible sources
FSC
www.fsc.org
FSC™ C018179

Penguin Books is committed to a sustainable
future for our business, our readers and our planet.
This book is made from Forest Stewardship
Council™ certified paper.

ALWAYS LEARNING   PEARSON

Contents

Introduction

Since then I have slowly learned to grasp how everything is connected across space and time, the life of the Prussian writer Kleist with that of a Swiss author who claims to have worked as a clerk in a brewery in Thun, the echo of a pistol shot across the Wannsee with the view from a window of the Herisau asylum, Walser's long walks with my own travels, dates of birth with dates of death, happiness with misfortune, natural history and the history of our industries, that of *Heimat* with that of exile. On all these paths Walser has been my constant companion. I only need to look up for a moment in my daily work to see him standing somewhere, a little apart, the unmistakable figure of the solitary walker just pausing to take in the surroundings.

What W. G. Sebald writes here, relating his first encounter with Robert Walser's short text on the dramatist Heinrich von Kleist's trip to Switzerland, 'Kleist in Thun', not only sets out *in nuce* his sense of affinity with Walser — indeed with all of the writers he discusses in this volume, to whom he wishes, as he claims in the Foreword, to 'pay my respects . . . before, perhaps, it may be too late' – but also seems to encapsulate the themes and preoccupations of this collection as a whole. That these themes and preoccupations overlap with those of Sebald's own creative works of 'prose fiction' (as he terms them) – *Vertigo*, *The Emigrants*, *The Rings of Saturn* and *Austerlitz* – is surely no coincidence, in view of the fact that the first three of these works already enjoyed considerable success at the time he composed the main part of these essays in 1997.

A Place in the Country was first published in German in 1998 under the title *Logis in einem Landhaus* (the title itself a quotation from Walser's 'Kleist in Thun'), which might be translated literally as 'lodgings in a country house' – or 'house in the country'. Shortly before that, Sebald's previous book, *The Rings of Saturn*, had appeared in English translation, having been published in German in 1995. In the meantime, following a visit to Corsica, he had commenced work on a book project relating to that island (which was, of course, the birthplace of Napoleon), a venture subsequently abandoned in favour of *Austerlitz*: extracts from the 'Korsika-Projekt', most of them previously published, appeared posthumously as essays in the volume *Campo Santo*. Traces of this Corsican project surface in the essays on Walser and Rousseau, as a kind of counterpoint to the Île Saint-Pierre, and it is tempting to conjecture that the essay on the philosopher from Geneva at least derives in part from that abandoned project. An interest in locality, then, notably rural and island locality, with its suggestions of being 'far from home', is a consistent feature of Sebald's work, and in these essays, with their loose structuring around an 'Alemannic' region comprising south-west Germany and north-west Switzer-land and Alsace, we may detect something of a 'Ritorno in patria', a kind of literary homecoming, after the 'English pilgrimage' of *The Rings of Saturn*, to the Alpine regions and their hinterlands traversed by the various protagonists of Sebald's first prose work, *Vertigo*. It is fitting, then, that the best-known of the Corsican essays in *Campo Santo* is entitled 'The Alps in the Sea'.

The six essays in the present volume have as their subjects six artists and writers, spanning, as the Foreword has it, a historical period of almost 200 years, from the Enlightenment and Roman-ticism in the eighteenth century – culminating in the French Revolution and the Napoleonic Wars – via Biedermeier quietism, the upheavals of 1848, the industrialization and colonialist expan-sionism of the nineteenth century, and the two World Wars of the twentieth; and although the rural idylls and writer's retreats they evoke might appear far removed from such historical turbulence, the seismic effects are registered even in the remotest of areas; among which one must count Sebald's native Allgäu. This moun-tainous region on the border with Austria belongs culturally and linguistically (as the name indeed suggests) to the 'Alemannic' area, referring to the group of dialects still spoken there, a direct descendant of the Middle High German of the *Minnesänger* – even though it is administratively now part of Bavaria, rather than Baden-Württemberg. While Johann Peter Hebel (1760–1826) comes from the Basel hinterland (in Baden), Eduard Mörike (1804–75) spent his life in the environs of Stuttgart in Swabia (Württemberg), and Sebald's contemporary from the Allgäu, the artist Jan Peter Tripp, now resides – as an earlier draft of the Foreword pointed out – in a *Landhaus* across the Rhine in Alsace. The other three authors are all Swiss, but here, as in *Vertigo*, the Alps which these regions border function not as a dividing but a unifying feature, so that the philosopher Jean-Jacques Rousseau (1712–78), across the linguistic boundary in Geneva, is linked to the Zurich-born Gottfried Keller (1819–90) and the peripatetic Robert Walser (1878–1956) – both writing in German – via the topography of the Île Saint-Pierre in the Lac de Bienne – or, as it is known in German, the St Petersinsel in the Bielersee – itself part of a bilingual region, and in many ways the heart of the book.

This intersection of languages and cultures in what is after all a region of many borders and transitions is reflected, too, in the fabric of Sebald's text, where, in keeping with the characteristic features of his creative prose, his carefully crafted German sentences are shot through with quotations and allusions, some French, some English, some even in Hebel's Alemannic dialect. There is, too, a hidden trajectory in the arrangement of the essays (which in this translation follows Sebald's own, not quite chronological, order in the German original). If it is from Fribourg, in French-speaking Switzerland, that the young student Sebald 'sets out for Manchester' in the autumn of 1966, symbolically placing Hebel's *Schatzkästlein*, Keller's *Der grüne Heinrich*, and Walser's *Jakob von Gunten* in his suitcase, then it is initially from Germany, or its southernmost tip, the Allgäu, that his journey 'far from home' begins. His first studies are in Freiburg im Breisgau, in Baden: the choice of a university in an 'Alemannic' area, rather than the arguably more obvious choice of the Bavarian capital Munich, seems significant. In moving away from the dialect world of the Southern Allgäu, with its Alemannic roots and inflections fondly remembered from his grandfather, 'whose use of language', as he writes, 'was in many ways reminiscent of that of the *Hausfreund*' (i.e. Johann Peter Hebel), he finds himself in the university environment of Freiburg, where, as he claims, only partly ironically, he had to learn to speak *Hochdeutsch* for the first time. From there he leaves Germany for the Université de Fribourg, in the French-speaking part of Switzerland – not far from Biel/Bienne (Robert Walser's birthplace) and the Île Saint-Pierre – and thence, as he tells us, to England, returning a year later to spend a year teaching in a private school at St Gallen in Switzerland, close to the asylum at Herisau where Robert Walser spent his final years.

W. G. Sebald's 'unwavering affection' for these authors, though, is not mere nostalgia, or a longing for a 'return to more innocent times'. Not only are their inflections, whether 'peripheral' South or Swiss German or Swiss-accented French, ones familiar to Sebald's ear, like the distinctive regional colouring of Hebel's prose, or the sheer quirkiness and inventiveness of Walser's use of language; so also are the crafting of the sentences, the unrolling of the narrative path, as he writes of Keller's *Der grüne Heinrich*, 'sentence after lovely sentence', and the poetic 'breaths and cadences' of that prose, which attract his attention both as a critic and a writer, as he explains to Michael Silverblatt in Los Angeles in one of his last interviews:

> The influence [on the rhythmic nature of his prose] came,
> if from anywhere, from nineteenth-century German prose

writing, which also has prosodic rhythms that *are* very pronounced, where prose is more important than, say, social background or plot in any manifest sense. And this nineteenth-century German prose writing even at the time was very provincial. It never was received outside Germany to any extent worth mentioning. But it's always been very close to me, not least because the writers all hailed from the periphery of the German-speaking lands, where I also come from. Adalbert Stifter in Austria, Gottfried Keller in Switzerland. They are both absolutely wonderful writers who achieved a very, very high intensity in their prose. [. . .] What they all have in common is this precedence of the carefully composed page of prose over the mechanisms of the novel such as dominated fiction writing elsewhere, in France and in England, notably, at that time.

These essays, then, offer us an unprecedented glimpse into the writer's workshop. In an early interview with Piet de Moor for the Belgian publication *Knack*, shortly after the first Dutch translation of *Vertigo*, Sebald explains how his writing 'involves a large number of much smaller tributes to other authors. These tributes take the form of citations that have casually crept into the text'; and this wry admission is echoed in *A Place in the Country*: 'I have always tried, in my own works, to mark my respect for those writers with whom I felt an affinity, to raise my hat to them, so to speak, by borrowing an attractive image or a few expressions . . .' What is more, his descriptions of their individual prose styles often seem to hint at an oblique comment on his own style of writing, as when he says of Hebel: 'The highly wrought language which Hebel devised especially for his almanac stories makes use of dialect and old-fashioned forms and turns of phrase precisely at those points where the rhythm of the prose demands it,' while noting Walser's 'painstaking process of elaboration', his 'playful – and sometimes obsessive – working in with a fine brush of the most abstruse details', or his use of 'regionalisms, redolent of things long fallen into disuse'. And even though the reluctant Swabian pastor Mörike does not perhaps evoke the same degree of affinity as the above writers, his work is compared to Schubert's music for its 'hidden shifts [. . .] those true *moments musicaux* where the iridescent chromatics begin to shimmer into dissonance, and an unexpected, even false change of key suddenly signals the abandoning of all hope, or, alternatively, grief gives way to consolation', giving rise to moments of pure limpidity such as are echoed in most of the essays here. Speculating as to how these are achieved leads W. G. Sebald to a consideration of the circumstances of the artist's life:

What it takes to produce these effects remains, now as then, an undisclosed mystery. Certainly a rare adeptness at their craft, permitting the most minute adjustments and nuances; and then, or so I imagine, a very long memory and, possibly, a certain unluckiness in love, which appears to have been precisely the lot of those who, like Mörike and Schubert, Keller and Walser, have bequeathed to us some few of the most beautiful lines ever written.

And so it is to the fateful compulsion of these tormented souls, their absolute failure to accommodate life and art, to which Sebald returns again and again, their fates resonating through time and space and the continued beauty of their surroundings, and forming a leitmotif common to all of the writers portrayed here – the description of the unhappiness and misfortunes of the writing subject being, of course, a constant theme of both Sebald's academic and his creative work.

If it is first and foremost as a fellow-writer, rather than as a scholar and critic, that the author of these essays addresses their subjects, the intersection we find here of creative and critical discourses is by no means a new phenomenon in W. G. Sebald's work. Articles on Ernst Herbeck and Franz Kafka published in the Austrian literary journal *Manuskripte* in the early 1980s parallel his literary engagement with these two figures in the fictional text *Vertigo* – though they are by no means the only writers to whom he 'pays tribute', there as elsewhere, by means of hidden quotations – while publication extracts from that work, such as episodes from the life of Stendhal, alternates in issues of *Manuskripte* with articles on these and other Austrian writers such as Adalbert Stifter, Peter Handke, and Gerhard Roth. The essays in *A Place in the Country* bring together – and share with his more overtly creative work – both the description of the misfortune of the writing subject, and the writer's sense of dislocation, whether in exile or in 'die fremdgewordene Heimat' (the home country grown strange), as he writes of the protagonists in Keller's 'A Village Romeo and Juliet'; in other words, the sense of being an 'expatriate' or 'emigrant' even, or especially, when at home. These preoccupations had indeed already formed the focus of Sebald's two earlier collections of academic essays and articles on Austrian literature 'from Stifter to Handke': *Die Beschreibung des Unglücks* (The Description of Misfortune) and *Unheimliche Heimat* (Strange Homeland), whose respective publication in 1985 and 1991, by the Austrian literary publishing house Residenz, frames that of Sebald's first two literary works, the long poem or 'Elementargedicht' *Nach der Natur (After Nature)* by Greno in 1988, and in 1990 *Schwindel. Gefühle (Vertigo)*, in the Eichborn series Die Andere Bibliothek, founded by Hans Magnus Enzensberger. In the same way, then, that the four stories which make up *The Emigrants* — like those in the earlier *Vertigo* — all have some apparently identifiable biographical basis, the pieces in the present volume trace a path between critical essay, life-writing, and creative writing. Both biographical 'narratives', and at the same time critical appreciations, they serve as examples of the way in which the critical interpretation of German literature (and in this case particularly Swiss and Alemannic or Swabian authors) informs and merges into the creative at all levels of Sebald's writing. At the same time the creative imagination is brought to bear upon the scholarly account of writers' lives, and the interpretation of their histories, in what one might almost term a 'natural history of creation'; an investigation of writers and their works in as it were their natural habitat, both in the context of the times in which they lived, as well as the physical landscapes that we see them traversing as solitary figures, often on foot.

In this, his first book with his new publisher, Hanser — followed in 1999 by *Luftkrieg und Literatur (On the Natural History of Destruction)* and in 2001 by *Austerlitz* – W. G. Sebald seems to have been determined to maintain the aesthetic standards of production set for his earlier literary works in Die Andere Bibliothek. Unlike the two earlier volumes of essays on Austrian literature (but in common with his works of prose fiction), it contains a wealth of images inserted into the text at key points; and it is worth noting that where Sebald's essays first appear in German or Swiss broadsheets – as a good many of them do – the texts are also often accompanied by illustrations, usually grainy photographs. Indeed, *A Place in the Country* goes further than the works of prose fiction in introducing not just double-paged image spreads, but inserted colour plates, which in the original (hardback) Hanser edition are designed to be folded out to the left or right of the facing text. Thus, as with the posthumous *Unrecounted* (*Unerzählt*), conceived in collaboration with Jan Peter Tripp, the book is not a mere collection of texts but appears to be envisaged as an aesthetic object in its own right, blurring not only the boundaries of the critical and the creative, but also those of the verbal and the visual.

Indeed, the first of these essays to be written was the one which forms a coda to the volume, on the paintings of Sebald's contemporary Jan Peter Tripp, which was originally published in 1993 in a catalogue of the latter's work entitled *Die Aufzählung der Schwierigkeiten* (The Enumeration of the Difficulties) – an allusion to which title, establishing a link between Tripp's work and his own methods, closes Sebald's Foreword: 'there are many difficulties to be reckoned with in the recollection [or, in homage to Michael Hamburger's translation of *Unrecounted*, 'recounting'] of things'. The remaining five essays were written during the course of 1997, as the dates on the manuscript in the Deutsches Literaturarchiv Marbach, in Sebald's characteristic Roman numerals, tell us, starting with the piece on Eduard Mörike, given as a speech on receipt of the *Mörike-Preis* in Fellbach (near the Swabian capital, Stuttgart) in April of that year, and subsequently published in association with that prize. There then follows the essay on Robert Walser, written in March, an extract of which was published in the *Neue Zürcher Zeitung* in May 1997; the pieces on Keller and Hebel are composed in June and July respectively, and the essay on Rousseau in August of that year (this last was published a year later, in a slightly different form and without any of the accompanying images, under the title 'Rousseau auf der Île de Saint-Pierre', in *Sinn und Form* in July/August 1998, shortly before the book's publication). The Foreword, finally, was added early in 1998.

Although the essays in this volume stand as individual pieces in their own right, they are nevertheless linked by 'a web of interlocking signs', motifs and images which recur from one essay to the next, linking, say, Hebel with Rousseau, Walser with Mörike, Keller with Tripp, whether via the obsessive attention to detail of the writer's (and artist's) craft, the predilection for small things and worlds in miniature, the unexpected mentions of Kleist and Hölderlin, or a boating trip across the water. This last, in particular, recurs in one form or another in almost all the essays, symbolic perhaps of the quest for a rural retreat, set apart from both the modern world and 'the hubbub of literary business' — even though such a retreat can only ever provide at best a temporary respite from the 'eternal business of cogitation' to which all writers, Sebald seems to suggest, are inexorably prone. This notwithstanding, in an interview with Arthur Lubow in 2001 Sebald describes his own visit to the Île Saint-Pierre – a visit which apparently inspired the essay on Rousseau – in the most idyllic, even nostalgic, of terms:

> I felt at home, strangely, because it is a miniature world. [. . .] One manor house, one farmhouse. A vineyard, a field of pota-toes, a field of wheat, a cherry tree, an orchard. It has one of everything, so it is in a sense an ark. It is like when you draw a place when you are a child. I don't like large-scale things, not in architecture or evolutionary leaps. I think it's an aberration. This notion of something that is small and self-contained is for me a moral and aesthetic ideal.

This artistic (and by implication moral) credo, a rejection of the relentless 'general expansionism' which so characterizes the onset of the modern age, is one which resonates throughout these essays. However, as readers of Sebald's fiction will know, he is always keenly aware of the vertiginous depths lurking 'beneath the surface illusionism', as he writes in the essay on Jan Peter Tripp. Of his fiction he remarks in the interview with Piet de Moor in 1992, pointing out the way that the 'beatific moments' serve to reveal the 'full measure of the horror', that

> the old-fashionedness of the diction or of the narrative tone is . . . nothing to do with nostalgia for a better age that's

gone past but is simply something that, as it were, heightens the awareness of that which we have managed to engineer in this century.

It is this awareness of the 'inherent contradiction between this nostalgic utopia and the inexorable march of progress towards the brink of the abyss', of the storm clouds always gathering on the historical and mental horizon, which renders so poignant and so precarious the perverse perseverance, the 'awful tenacity' as Sebald says in the Foreword, of those who devote their lives to literature, 'the hapless writers trapped in their web of words', who, in spite of everything, nevertheless 'sometimes succeed in opening up vistas of such beauty and intensity as life itself is scarcely able to provide'.

Jo Catling
Norwich, January 2013

Foreword

I t is a good thirty years since I first became acquainted with the writers who are the subjects of the essays in this volume. I can still remember quite clearly how, when I set out from Switzerland for Manchester in the early autumn of 1966, I placed Gottfried Keller's *Der grüne Heinrich*, Johann Peter Hebel's *Schatzkästlein des Rheinischen Hausfreunds*, and a disintegrating copy of Robert Walser's *Jakob von Gunten* in my suitcase.* The countless pages I have read since then have done nothing to diminish my appreciation of these books and their authors, and if today I were obliged to move again to another island, I am sure they would once again find a place in my luggage. This unwavering affection for Hebel, Keller and Walser was what gave me the idea that I should pay my respects to them before, perhaps, it may be too late. The two pieces on Rousseau and Mörike had their origins elsewhere, but as it turns out they are by no means out of place in this context. The essays in this volume span a period of almost 200 years – which goes to show how little has altered, in all this time, when it comes to that peculiar behavioural disturbance which

---

* Gottfried Keller, *Der grüne Heinrich* (*Green Henry*); Johann Peter Hebel, *Schatzkästlein des Rheinischen Hausfreunds* (*Treasure Chest of the Rhineland Family Friend*); Robert Walser, *Jakob von Gunten* (*Jakob von Gunten / Institute Benjamenta*). Publication details of these and other texts and their English translations are given in the Bibliography.

causes every emotion to be transformed into letters on the page and which bypasses life with such extraordinary precision. What I found most surprising in the course of these observations is the awful tenacity of those who devote their lives to writing. There seems to be no remedy for the vice of literature; those afflicted persist in the habit despite the fact that there is no longer any pleasure to be derived from it, even at that critical age when, as Keller remarks, one every day runs the risk of becoming simple-minded, and longs for nothing more than to put a halt to the wheels ceaselessly turning in one's head. Rousseau, who in his refuge on the Île Saint-Pierre – he is fifty-three years old at this point – already longs for an end to the eternal business of cogitation, nevertheless keeps on writing up to the very end. Mörike, too, carries on tinkering with his novel long after it has ceased to be worth the trouble. Keller retires at fifty-six from his official position as civil servant in order to surrender himself completely to his literary work, and Walser can only free himself from the obsessive compulsion to write by as it were disenfranchising himself and withdrawing from society altogether. In view of this drastic measure, watching a French television documentary a few months ago I was profoundly moved by a remark by a former orderly from the asylum at Herisau, one Josef Wehrle, who related how Walser, despite having completely turned his back on literature, would always carry with him in his waistcoat pocket a pencil stub and a few scraps of paper, carefully cut to size, on which he would often jot down one thing or another. However, Josef Wehrle continued, Walser was always quick to conceal these scraps of paper if he thought anyone was watching, as if he had been caught in the act of doing something wrong, or even shameful. Evidently the business of writing is one from whose clutches it is by no means easy to extricate oneself, even when the activity itself has come to seem loathsome or even impossible. From the writer's point of view, there is almost nothing to be said in its defence, so little does it have to offer by way of gratification. Perhaps it would really be better simply to set down – as Keller originally intended – a brief novel with the career of a young artist tragically cut short, and a cypress-dark ending that sees everyone dead and buried, before laying aside the pen for good. The reader, though, would stand to lose much thereby, for the hapless writers trapped in their web of words sometimes succeed in opening up vistas of such beauty and intensity as life itself is scarcely able to provide. And so it is as a reader, first and foremost, that I wish to pay tribute to these colleagues who have gone before me, in the form of these extended marginal notes and glosses, which do not otherwise have any particular claim to make. That the final essay has a painter as its subject is also right and proper, not merely because for quite some time Jan Peter Tripp and I went to school together in Oberstdorf, and because Keller and Walser mean a great deal to both of us, but also because from his pictures I have learned how it is essential to gaze far beneath the surface, that art is nothing without patient handiwork, and that there are many difficulties to be reckoned with in the recollection of things.[1]

A Comet in the Heavens

A piece for an almanac, in honour of
Johann Peter Hebel

In the feuilleton which Walter Benjamin wrote for the *Magdeburger Zeitung* on the centenary of the death of Johann Peter Hebel, he suggests near the beginning that the nineteenth century cheated itself of the realization that the *Schatzkästlein des Rheinischen Hausfreunds* [*Treasure Chest of the Rhineland Family Friend*] is one of the purest examples of prose writing in all of German literature.[1] Out of a misplaced sense of cultural superiority, the key to this casket was thrown among peasants and children, heedless of the treasures concealed within. Indeed, between Goethe's and Jean Paul's praise of the almanac author from Baden and the later appreciation of his work by Kafka, Bloch and Benjamin, we find scarcely anyone who might have introduced Hebel to a bourgeois readership, and thus shown them what they were missing in terms of a vision of a better world designed with the ideals of justice and tolerance in mind. It says something, too, about German intellectual history if we consider what little impact the intercession of these Jewish authors of the 1910s and 1920s had on Hebel's

7

posthumous reputation, by comparison with the effect the National Socialists had when they later laid claim to the *Heimatschriftsteller* [local or provincial writer] from Wiesenthal for their own purposes. With what false neo-Germanic accents this expropriation took place, and how long it was to prevail, is clearly set out by Robert Minder in his essay on Heidegger's 1957 lecture on Hebel,[2] the whole tenor and expression of which differed not in the slightest from that employed during the Nazi era by Josef Weinheber, Guido Kolbenheyer, Hermann Burte, Wilhelm Schäfer and other would-be guardians of the German heritage, who fondly imagined that their jargon was rooted directly in the language of the *Volk*. When I commenced my studies in Freiburg in 1963, all that had only just been swept under the carpet, and since then I have often wondered how dismal and distorted our appreciation of literature might have remained, had not the gradually appearing writings of Walter Benjamin and the Frankfurt School – which was, in effect, a Jewish school for the investigation of bourgeois social and intellectual history – provided an alternative perspective. In my own case, at any rate, without the assistance of Bloch[3] and Benjamin I should scarcely have found my way to Hebel at all through the Heideggerian fog. Now, though, I return time and time again to the *Kalendergeschichten* [*Calendar* or *Almanac Stories*], possibly because, as Benjamin also noted, a seal of their perfection is that they are so easy to forget. But it is not just the ethereal and ephemeral nature of Hebel's prose which every few weeks makes me want to check whether the Barber of Segringen and the Tailor of Penza are still there; what always

8

draws me back to Hebel is the completely coincidental fact that my grandfather, whose use of language was in many ways reminiscent of that of the *Hausfreund*, would every year buy a

1956 Wochen- u. Monatstage	II. FEBRUAR Namens- und Festtage	Lauf / Alter	oder Tau-Monat hat 29 Tage. Planetenschein	Mondsbrüche
Mittw. 1	Ignaz, Brigida, Siegbert			☾ Letztes Viertel
Donn. 2	Maria Lichtmeß Kornelius			a. 3. u. 1 7 Uhr 8 Min.
Freitag 3	A. Blasius, Oskar, (14 M.)			2. Wachsweihe
Samst. 4	Andreas Corsini, Veronika			3. Halssegnung
6.	**Vom Sämann und guten Samen. Luk. 8, 4—15. Tageslänge 9 Std. 40 Min.**			
Sonnt. 5	Sexagesima Agatha, Alwin			5. Brotweihe
Montag 6	Dorothea, Amandus, Titus			● Neumond am
Dienst. 7	Richard, Theodor, Romuald			11. um 22 Uhr 38
Mittw. 8	Johann von Matha Ordst.			Min. Nach zeitwei=
Donn. 9	Apollonia, Cyrill, Alto Abt			sem Aufklaren wie=
Freitag 10	A. Scholastika, Wilhelm			der unfreundlich und
Samst. 11	Euphrosine, Adolf, Maria Erschein. zu Lourdes			ziemlich kalt.
7.	**Von der Verkündigung seines Leidens. Luk. 18, 31—43. Tagesl. 10 Std. 1 Min.**			
Sonnt. 12	Quinqu. Eulalia J. u. M.			15. Aschenweihe
Montag 13	Katharina v. R., Ermenhild			☽ Erstes Viertel
Dienst. 14	Fasnacht Valentin, Anton			am 19. um 10 Uhr
Mittw. 15	F.A. Ascherm. Siegfried			der Kälte und viel
Donn. 16	Juliana M., Gregor X. P.			Regen.
Freitag 17	F.A. Donatus, Fintanus			
Samst. 18	Simeon M., Flavian M.			18. Osterbeicht-Anfang
8.	**Von der Versuchung Jesu. Matth. 4, 1—11. Tageslänge 10 Std. 25 Min.**			
Sonnt. 19	1. Invoc. Konrad v. Piac.			19. Funkensonntag
Montag 20	Eleutherius B., Eucherius			
Dienst. 21	Eleonora Königin, Felix B.			○ Vollmond er=
Mittw. 22	F. I. Quat. Petri Stuhlfeier			gänzt täglich am 26. um
Donn. 23	Milburga Abtissin, Willigis			2 Uhr 41 Minuten.
Freitag 24	F.A. Schalttag			Rauh und windig.
Samst. 25	F. Marthias Ap., Edilbert			
9.	**Von der Verklärung Christi. Matth. 17, 1—9. Tageslänge 10 Std. 49 Min.**			
Sonnt. 26	2. Remin. Walburga, Felix			Wenn's der Hornung
Montag 27	Dionys v. Augsb., Ottokar			gnädig macht,
Dienst. 28	Leander, Renate, Baldomer			bringt der Lenz
Mittw. 29	Roman, Oswald, Martin			den Frost bei Nacht.

Wenn es an Lichtmeß stürmt und schneit, ist der Frühling nicht mehr weit,
ist es aber klar und hell, kommt der Lenz noch nicht so schnell.
Wenn's im Hornung nicht tüchtig schneit, so kommt die Kälte zur Osterzeit.
Schmilzt die Sonne im Februar die Butter, geben die Wiesen spätes Futter.

Kempter Calender [Kempten Almanac], in which he would note, in his indelible pencil, the name days of his relatives and friends, the first frost, the first snowfall, the onset of the *Föhn*, thunderstorms, hailstorms and suchlike, and also, on the pages

1.
2.
3.
4.
5.
6.
7.
8.
9.
10.
11.
12.
13.
14.
15.
16.
17.
18.
19.
20.
21.
22.
23.
24.
25.
26.
27.
28.
29.

5

left blank for notes, the occasional recipe for *Wermuth*[4] or for gentian schnapps. Naturally, by the 1950s the stories in the *Kempter Calender* – which first appeared in 1773 – by authors such as Franz Schrönghamer-Heimdahl and Else Eberhard-Schobacher, telling of a shepherd lad from the Lechtal or a skeleton discovered in

the Bergwald, did not quite live up to the quality of Hebel's own *Kalendergeschichten*, but the basic format of the Almanac had by and large remained the same, and the multiplication tables, the tables for calculating rates of interest, the saints' names beside every date, the Sundays and holy days marked in red, the phases of the moon,

Zins-Berechnungen.

Kapital Betrag	Zu 2 Prozent			Zu 3 Prozent			Zu 3½ Prozent			Zu 4 Prozent			Zu 4½ Prozent			Zu 5 Prozent		
Mark	1 Tag Pf.	1 Mon. M.Pf.	1 Jahr M.Pf.	1 Tag Pf.	1 Mon. M.Pf.	1 Jahr M.Pf.	1 Tag Pf.	1 Mon. M.Pf.	1 Jahr M.Pf.	1 Tag Pf.	1 Mon. M.Pf.	1 Jahr M.Pf.	1 Tag Pf.	1 Mon. M.Pf.	1 Jahr M.Pf.	1 Tag Pf.	1 Mon. M.Pf.	1 Jahr M.Pf.
10	—	—.2	—.20	—	—.3	—.30	—	—.3	—.35	—	—.3	—.40	—	—.4	—.45	—	—.4	—.50
20	—	—.3	—.40	—	—.5	—.60	—	—.6	—.70	—	—.6	—.80	—	—.7	—.90	—	—.8	1.—
30	—	—.5	—.60	—	—.7	—.90	—	—.9	1.05	—	—.10	1.20	—	—.11	1.35	—	—.12	1.50
40	—	—.7	—.80	—	—.10	1.20	—	—.12	1.40	—	—.13	1.60	—	—.15	1.80	—	—.17	2.—
50	—	—.8	1.—	—	—.12	1.50	—	—.14	1.75	—	—.17	2.—	—	—.19	2.25	—	—.21	2.50
60	—	—.10	1.20	—	—.15	1.80	—	—.17	2.10	1	—.20	2.40	1	—.23	2.70	1	—.25	3.—
70	—	—.12	1.40	—	—.17	2.10	1	—.20	2.45	1	—.23	2.80	1	—.26	3.15	1	—.29	3.50
80	—	—.13	1.60	—	—.20	2.40	1	—.23	2.80	1	—.27	3.20	1	—.30	3.60	1	—.33	4.—
90	—	—.15	1.80	1	—.22	2.70	1	—.26	3.15	1	—.30	3.60	1	—.34	4.05	1	—.38	4.50
100	—	—.17	2.—	1	—.25	3.—	1	—.29	3.50	1	—.33	4.—	1	—.38	4.50	1	—.42	5.—
200	1	—.33	4.—	2	—.50	6.—	2	—.58	7.—	2	—.67	8.—	2	—.75	9.—	3	—.83	10.—
300	2	—.50	6.—	2	—.75	9.—	3	—.87	10.50	3	1.—	12.—	4	1.12	13.50	4	1.25	15.—
400	2	—.67	8.—	3	1.—	12.—	4	1.16	14.—	4	1.33	16.—	5	1.50	18.—	5	1.67	20.—
500	3	—.83	10.—	4	1.25	15.—	5	1.46	17.50	6	1.67	20.—	6	1.87	22.50	7	2.08	25.—
600	3	1.—	12.—	5	1.50	18.—	6	1.75	21.—	7	2.—	24.—	8	2.25	27.—	8	2.50	30.—
700	4	1.17	14.—	6	1.75	21.—	7	2.04	24.50	8	2.33	28.—	9	2.62	31.50	10	2.92	35.—
800	4	1.33	16.—	7	2.—	24.—	8	2.33	28.—	9	2.67	32.—	10	3.—	36.—	11	3.33	40.—
900	5	1.50	18.—	7	2.25	27.—	9	2.62	31.50	10	3.—	36.—	11	3.38	40.50	12	3.75	45.—
1000	5	1.67	20.—	8	2.50	30.—	10	2.92	35.—	11	3.33	40.—	12	3.75	45.—	14	4.17	50.—

Bei höheren Zinssätzen sind die Zahlen je nachdem zu teilen, oder zu vervielfältigen.

the symbols of the planets and signs of the Zodiac, and the Jewish calendar, which strangely enough was still retained even after

Kalender der Juden
für das 5716te in das 5717te Jahr der Welt.

5716	(Langes Gemeinjahr 355 Tg.)	1956	5716		1956
Schebat 1.	. . . .	Januar 14.	Ab 9.	Fasten, Tempel=Verbr.	Juli 17.
Adar 1.	. . . .	Februar 13.	Elul 1.	. . . .	August 8.
" 11.	Fasten=Esther . . .	" 23.	**5717**		
" 14.	Purim . . .	" 26.	Tischri	(Langes Schaltjahr 385 Tage)	
" 15.	Schuschan=Purim . . .	" 27.	1.	Neujahrsfest*	Sept. .
Nisan 1.	. . . .	März 13.	2.	Zweites Fest*	" .
" 15.	Passah=Fest* (Ostern)	" 27.	3.	Fasten=Gedaljah	" 9.
" 16.	Zweites Fest*	" 28.	10.	Versöhnungsfest*	" 15.
" 21.	Siebentes Fest*	April 2.	15.	Laubhüttenfest*	" 20.
" 22.	Achtes Fest*	" 3.	16.	Zweites Fest*	" .
Ijar 1.	. . . .	" 12.	21.	Palmenfest . . .	" 10.
" 18.	(Lag=B'omer Schülerf.)	" 29.	22.	Laubhüttenfestende* .	" 27.
Sivan 1.	. . . .	Mai 11.	23.	Gesetzesfreude* . .	" 28.
" 6.	(Wochenfest* Pfingsten)	" 16.	Marchesch. 1.	. . . .	Oktober 6.
" 7.	Zweites Fest*	" 17.	Kislev 1.		Nov. 5.
Thamuz 1.	. . . .	Juni 10.	25.	Tempelweihe . . .	" 29.
" 17.	Fasten, Tempel=Erob.	" 26.	Tebet 1.		Dezbr. 5.
Ab 1.	. . . .	Juli 9.	10.	Fasten, Belag. Jerusal.	" 14.

Die mit * bezeichneten Feste werden streng gefeiert.

1945 – all this even today constitutes for me a system in which, as once in my childhood, I would still like to imagine that everything

Rötteln Castle and Village with the Wiesental,
oil painting by Heinrich Reichelt

is arranged for the best. For this reason, nowhere do I find the idea of a world in perfect equilibrium more vividly expressed than in what Hebel writes about the cultivation of fruit trees, of the flowering of the wheat,[5] of a bird's nest or of the different kinds of rain; nowhere more readily grasped than when I observe the way in which, with his unerring moral compass, he differentiates between gratitude and ingratitude, avarice and extravagance, and all the various other vices and frailties mankind is heir to. Against the blind and headlong onrush of history he sets occasions when misfortune endured is recompensed; where every military campaign is followed by a peace treaty, and every puzzle has a solution; and in the book of Nature which Hebel spreads open before us we may observe how even the most curious of creatures, such as the processionary caterpillars and the flying fish, each has its place in the most carefully balanced order. Hebel's wonderful inner certainty is derived, though, less from what he knows about the nature of things than from the contemplation of that which surpasses rational thought. Doubtless his continued observations about the cosmos were intended to give his readers a gentle introduction to the universe, to make it familiar so that they may imagine that on the most distant stars, as they glisten in the night like the lights of a strange town, people like us are sitting in their living rooms at home 'and reading the newspaper, or saying their evening prayers, or else are spinning and knitting, or playing a game of trumps, while the young lad is working out a mathematical problem using the rule of three'; and certainly Hebel describes for us the orbits of the planets, noting for our edification how long a cannonball fired in Breisach would take to reach Mars, and speaks of the moon as our most trusted guardian, true household friend and the first maker of calendars of this earth; yet his true art lies in the inversion of this perspective encompassing even the furthest stars, when from the point of view of an extraterrestrial being he looks out into the glittering heavens, and from there sees our sun as a tiny star, and the earth not at all, and suddenly no longer knows 'that there was a war on in Austria and that the Turks won the siege of Silistria'. Ultimately it is this cosmic perspective, and the insights derived from it into our own insignificance, which is the source of the sovereign serenity with which Hebel presides in his stories over the vagaries of human destiny. Such moments of stopping to stare, in pure contemplation, give rise to his most profound inspiration. 'Have we not all,' he writes, 'seen the Milky Way, which encircles the heavens like a broad, floating girdle? It resembles an eternal wreath of mist, shot through by a palely gleaming light. But viewed through an astronomer's lens, this whole cloud of light resolves itself into innumerable tiny stars, as when one gazes out of the window at a mountain and sees nothing but green, yet looking even through an ordinary field-glass one can make out tree upon tree, and leaf upon leaf, and gives up counting altogether.' Rational thought is stilled, and the bourgeois instinct – otherwise so favoured by Hebel – with its passion for cataloguing everything no longer stirs. By often thus abandoning himself to pure contemplation and wonderment, with subtle irony our *Hausfreund* undermines his own proclaimed omniscience at every turn. Indeed, despite his professional didactic inclinations, he never takes up a central role as preceptor, but always positions himself slightly to one side, in the same manner as ghosts, a number of whom inhabit his stories, who are known for their habit of observing life from their marginal position in silent puzzlement and resignation. Once one has become aware of the way Hebel accompanies his characters as a faithful *compagnon*, it is almost possible to read his remarks on the comet which appeared in 1 8 1 1 as a self-portrait. 'Did it not every night,' writes Hebel, 'appear like a blessing in the evening sky, or like a priest when he walks around the church sprinkling holy water, or, so to speak, like a good and noble friend of the earth who looks back at her wistfully, as if it had wanted to say: I was once an earth like you, full of snow-flurries and thunderclouds, hospitals and Rumford's soup-kitchens and cemeteries. But my Day of Judgement has passed and has transfigured me in heavenly light, and I would fain come down to you, but I may not, lest I become sullied again by the blood of your battlefields. It did not say that, but it seemed so, for it became ever brighter and more lovely, the nearer it came, more generous and more joyful, and as it moved away it grew pale and melancholy, as if it too took this to heart.' Both, the comet and the narrator, draw their train of light across our lives disfigured by violence, observing everything going on below, but from the greatest distance imaginable. The strange constellation, in which sympathy and indifference are elided, is as it were the professional secret of the chronicler, who sometimes covers a whole century on a single page, and yet keeps a watchful eye on even the most insignificant circumstances, who does not speak of poverty in general but describes how back at home the children's nails are blue with hunger, and who senses that there is some unfathomable connection between, for example, the domestic squabbles of a married couple in Swabia and the loss of an entire army in the floodwaters of the Berezina. If the essence of Hebel's epic world view is the result of a particular disposition and receptiveness of the soul, then the way it is conveyed to the reader, too, has a flavour all its own. 'When the French army was encamped across the Rhine after the retreat from Germany . . .'; 'after she had left Basel by postchaise via the St Johannistor and had passed the vineyards on the way into the Sundgau . . .'; 'just as the sun was setting over the mountains in Alsace . . .': in such manner the stories progress. As one thing follows another, so, very gradually, the narrative unfolds. Nevertheless, the language constantly checks itself, holding itself up in small loops and digressions and moulding itself to that which it describes, along the way recuperating as many earthly goods as it possibly can. Hebel's narrative style is characterized further by his intermittent borrowings from dialect, of both vocabulary and word order. 'For to count the stars there's not fingers enough in the whole world,'[6] it says in the syntax of Baden or Alsace at the beginning of a piece in the 'Betrachtungen des Weltgebäudes' [Observations concerning the Cosmos], and in the piece about the Great Sanhedrin in Paris we read: 'The great Emperor Napoleon accepted this, and in the year 1806, before he began the great journey to Jena, Berlin and Warsaw, and Eylau, he had letters be sent to all the Jews in France that they should from among their midst send him men of sense and learning from all the departments of the Empire.'[7] The words are, in this sentence,[8] not set down in accordance with Alemannic usage, but rather follow exactly the word order of Yiddish, which refuses to subordinate itself to the rules of German syntax.[9] This fact alone ought to be enough to refute the primitive Heideggerian thesis of

Hebel's rootedness in the native soil of the *Heimat*. The highly wrought language which Hebel devised especially for his stories in the Almanac makes use of dialect and old-fashioned forms and turns of phrase precisely at those points where the rhythm of the prose demands it, and probably functioned even in his own day more as a distancing effect than as a badge of tribal affiliation. Nor is Hebel's particular fondness for the paratactic conjunctions 'and', 'or' and 'but' necessarily indicative of a homespun *naïveté*; rather, it is precisely the way he deploys these particles which gives rise to some of his most sophisticated effects. Opposed to any hierarchy or subordination, they suggest to the reader in the most unobtrusive way that, in the world created and administered by this narrator, everything has an equal right to coexist alongside everything else. The pilgrim promises to bring the landlady of the Baselstab a shell 'from the seashore of Ascalon' on his return, or a rose of Jericho. And the journeyman's apprentice from Duttlingen says at the graveside of the merchant from Amsterdam, more to himself than to the latter, 'Poor Kannitverstan, what use are all your riches to you now? No more than my poverty will bring me one day: a shroud and a winding-sheet; and of all your lovely flowers a bunch of rosemary perhaps upon your cold breast or a sprig of rue.' In these cadences and inflections at the end of a sentence, which mark the profoundest emotional moments in Hebel's prose, it is as if the language turns in upon itself, and we can almost feel the narrator's hand upon our arm. This sense of *fraternité* can be realized – far from any thought of actual social equality – only against the horizon of eternity, whose other side is the gold background against which, as Walter Benjamin noted, the chroniclers love to paint their characters.[10] In these seemingly inconclusive final clauses, ending as it were on a half-note and trailing away into nothingness, Hebel rises above the concerns and considerations of the world and assumes a vantage point from where, as it says in a note in Jean Paul's *Nachlaß*, one can look down on mankind's distant promised land – that home, in fact, where, according to another saying, no one has ever been.[11]

Hebel's cosmographical observations are an attempt, in the clear light of reason, to lift the veil which separates us from the world beyond. *Weltfrömmigkeit* [secular piety][12] and the study of nature take the place of faith and metaphysics. The perfect mechanism of the spheres is, for the Almanac author, proof of the existence of a realm of light which we may at the last enter upon. Hebel permitted himself no doubts upon this matter; indeed, his office clearly precluded such a possibility. But in his dreams – beyond the reach of the controlling authority of consciousness – which for a while he was in the habit of writing down, we find not a few indications that he too was prey to troubling fears and insecurities. 'I was lying,' he notes on the 5th of November 1805, 'in my old bedroom in my mother's house. There was an oak tree growing in the middle of the room. The room had no ceiling, and the tree reached up into the rafters. In places the tree was aflame, which was most lovely to look at. Finally the flames reached the uppermost branches and the roof-beams began to catch fire. After the fire had been extinguished, a greenish resin-like substance, which later became gelatinous, was found at the seat of the fire, as well as a great number of ugly dirty-green beetles gnawing greedily at it.' Just as alarming as this transformation of the nursery with its glowing

Christmas tree into a place teeming with horror is the dream image of the damned souls in hell, where in the shape of hot fishes and other sea creatures they lie among beech leaves in a warm room.[13] Indeed, for Hebel the animal kingdom in general appears rather disturbing: whether it is the tiny mouse with a sky-blue patch on its back which hops around under his feet, or the African lion which enters his room and places its forepaws, disfigured by mange, on his shoulders — not to mention the pair of angels, one a pregnant female, who are kept in a chicken run together with the other domestic fowl. Proving his identity is something which also variously troubles Hebel in his dreams; one night he is seated at table with Christ and the Apostles, and fears that they will notice that he is not quite kosher in his beliefs, and on another occasion he is unmasked as a spy in Paris and denies his origins. The surreal world of dreams, then, is far from the star-strewn Elysian Fields which Hebel creates by day in his imagination, pen in hand. The random and arbitrary way in which the most incongruous things are combined there may be seen as a reaction to an era when the last remnants of the medieval view of a divinely ordered universe were being torn asunder, while at the same time secular history, in the form of endless wars and revolutions, was beginning everywhere to extend its violent reach. The superstition that the appearance of a comet in the heavens was a portent of impending disaster our Almanac author, characteristically, dismisses lightly with the remark that unfortunately the number of calamitous events occurring between 1789 and 1810 exceeded by far the occurrence of stars with tails. 'You, gentle reader,' he writes, 'need only look back at the last twenty years, at all the revolutions and trees of liberty, the sudden death of Emperor Leopold, the death met by King Louis XVI, the assassination of the Turkish emperor, the bloody wars in Germany, the Netherlands, in Switzerland, Italy, Poland, Spain, the battles of Austerlitz and Eylau, at Esslingen[14] and Wagram; at the outbreaks of yellow fever, typhus and cattle plagues, the conflagrations in Copenhagen, Stockholm and Constantinople, and the rising cost of coffee and sugar' in order to understand that one can never know, first thing in the morning, what will happen by nightfall. The prime example of this is *Das Unglück der Stadt Leiden* [The Catastrophe of the City of Leiden],[15] where life is going on as usual despite the fact that a ship laden with seventy barrels of gunpowder is lying at anchor in the harbour. 'People were having their midday meal, enjoying it as they do every day, even though the ship was still there. But in the afternoon when the clock on the big tower stood at four-thirty – industrious people were sitting at home working, devout mothers were cradling their infants, merchants were going about their business, children were gathered for their evening lessons, people of leisure had time on their hands and were sitting in the inn with a game of cards and a jug of wine, a man full of care was worrying about the morrow, how he would eat, drink, clothe himself, and a thief was maybe just inserting a counterfeit key into someone else's door – and suddenly there was an almighty bang. The ship with its seventy barrels of gunpowder caught fire and exploded, and in one instant whole long streets of houses with all that lived and dwelled in them were blown to pieces and collapsed into a pile of rubble or were damaged most terribly. Many hundreds of people were buried dead and alive under these ruins or gravely injured. Three schools and all the children in them were destroyed, people and animals who were outdoors in the vicinity of the disaster were thrown into the air by the force of the blast and came down to earth in a pitiable state. To make matters worse a conflagration broke out which was soon raging everywhere and could scarcely be extinguished, as many warehouses full of oil and blubber also went up in flames. Eight hundred beautiful buildings collapsed or had to be demolished.' In his evocation of the destruction of the city of Leiden, Hebel as it were sums up the experience of an entire epoch. Born in 1760, he lived through the collapse of the *ancien régime* just across the border in France, the outbreak of the Revolution, the years of the Terror, and the pan-European wars which followed, as a catastrophic escalation and headlong precipitation of history. Nowhere in Hebel's work – not the story of the disaster visited upon the Dutch city of Leiden, nor anywhere else in his writing – is there any evidence to suggest that he sympathized with the endemic political violence erupting everywhere in Europe between 1789 and 1814. Walter Benjamin's wishful conjecture, that Hebel might have seen the French Revolution as an act of divine reason intervening in human history, is based – as Hannelore Schlaffer shows in the afterword to her beautifully illustrated edition of the *Schatzkästlein* [*Treasure Chest*] – on an imprecise historical perspective which 'confused the revolutionary turmoils on the Upper Rhine in the 1790s with the reforms of the early years of the nineteenth century'. Robert Minder, too – the most reliable witness in these matters – points out that Hebel only supported the Revolution, if at all, in its most restrained and liberal form. And the *Hausfreund* himself, in 1815, once the upheavals finally appear to have died down, tells his readers *expressis verbis* that he has never yet sported a cockade. Although hedged about with all kinds of ironies, this retrospective declaration on Hebel's part is surely not to be ascribed to opportunistic motives, since at no point were his hopes and philosophy directed at a violent and bloody reversal of the status quo. His concern was only ever for the practical improvement of the living conditions of the people, such as was promoted by Karl Friedrich, Grand Duke of Baden, beginning with his abolition of serfdom in a decree of the 23rd of July 1783, in the consequent reforms in education and health provision, of agriculture and administration, as well as by the local Baden adaptation of the Napoleonic *Code Civil*. Karl Friedrich was a follower of the French physiocrats, whose principal advocates, François Quesnay and Jean Claude Marie Vincent, sought, in the face of the far-reaching changes affecting collective life in the eighteenth century, to achieve a lasting basis for a harmonization of society based upon natural law. Accordingly, the centrepiece of their economic philosophy was agriculture, which they saw as the only true form of production and of decisive importance for the common good. The processing of raw materials in manufacture, trade and industry represented, for them, enterprises of a secondary nature. Simultaneously progressive and conservative, the physiocrats' philosophy was determined by the attempt as it were to inculcate a bourgeois sense of rationality in the prevailing aristocratic regime, and by this means to protect it from precisely that end which was already inevitable, should it fail to replace the more or less ruthless exploitation of its inherited resources by a more enlightened practice. The ideal the physiocrats had in mind was of a country resembling a large and flourishing garden. Hannelore

Schlaffer quotes a Zurich city doctor of the mid eighteenth century who was of the opinion that there would be no deceit and no violence, and everywhere peace and satisfaction would reign, 'if only all men would cultivate the fields and provide for themselves by the work of their hands'.[16] In such nostalgic utopian views was the educated middle class wont to articulate its discomfiture at the rapid spread of the economy of goods and capital it had itself created, and which was now proliferating year on year. The adherents of the physiocratic school believed that the realization of their 'natural' order of society could most readily be achieved within a state ruled by means of a so-called loyal despotism, which would enable their ideas for reform to be put directly into practice. Besides concurring with the substance of their ideas, it was this political line which meant that it made sense for a ruler like Karl Friedrich to follow the precepts of the physiocrats. As far as Hebel is concerned, it was in the benevolent regime of Karl Friedrich – and certainly not in the Revolution, transforming as it did a process of reform into a calamity – that he saw the blueprint for realizing a better future for human society. In the manner of a wise and benevolent monarch, so too the *Hausfreund* performs his office of narrator. The stories and reports he presents, the lessons he imparts, and all the other things he elaborates on in the all-embracing natural order, taken together add up to a kind of Solomonic manual for the lower orders, as well as a treatise on statescraft in which the local ruler may see himself reflected in role models intended not least as a guide to the proper fulfilment of the task entrusted to him by the grace of God. In this respect, Hebel's political position is closely related to the one Goethe adopts in his *Novelle*, which of course is concerned with averting the dangers of fire (in other words revolution) by means of a feudal system of government, which is nevertheless imbued with a bourgeois work ethic and sense of duty. Whereas Goethe, though, very nearly makes his young prince into a shining example of the new spirit of enterprise, whose main principle is 'that one receives more than one gives', Hebel, when talking of Kaiser Joseph, Frederick the Great, the clever Sultan, or the Tsar of Russia, prefers to hold fast to the tried and tested paternalistic system where any intervention on the part of the *Landesväter* or local sovereigns in the lives of their subjects invariably turns out to be a blessing. Nowhere in Hebel do we detect even the slightest hint of irreverence. Goodness and justice are the lodestars of the paternalistic order, the unquestioning acceptance of which is nowhere better illustrated than in the many variations on the set pieces in which the ruling prince goes unrecognized as he mingles amongst the people. Our Almanac author too presents us with a number of these, perhaps most strikingly in the story from 1809 which relates how Napoleon did not neglect to discharge his longstanding debt to the fruit woman in Brienne. In order that the reader may see the matter in its proper perspective, the *Hausfreund* merely sketches in the stages of Napoleon's career since his time as a cadet in the military school at Brienne. 'Soon,' he writes, 'Napoleon was made a general and conquered Italy. Napoleon went to Egypt where the children of Israel once made bricks and he fought a battle near Nazareth where the blessed virgin lived eighteen hundred years ago. Napoleon sailed straight back to France over a sea swarming with enemy ships, arrived in Paris and became First Consul. Napoleon restored peace and law and order to the troubled country and became French Emperor.' And a few lines after the recapitulation of this meteoric career we see the Emperor, incognito like one of these legendary righteous souls who hold the world in equilibrium, stepping through a narrow door into the room in which the fruit woman is just preparing her frugal supper. One thousand two hundred francs capital and interest are counted out on to his creditor's table, so that henceforth she will be provided for, and her children too, of whom one might now almost say he thought of as his own.

If the Emperor's visit to the fruit woman as evening falls already has about it something of an echo of the Annunciation, then the description of his astonishing ascent is even richer in biblical associations. There is talk of the exile of the children of Israel, of the Holy Land and the blessed Virgin, and, perhaps most important of all, of the return of a youthful hero across a sea full of enemy ships, bringing with him peace and a new order. The messianic calling is unmistakable, and clearly takes precedence over the claims of the ancient ruling houses, to whom Napoleon, as is well known, gave somewhat short shrift. For a while at least, then, Hebel's political hopes too were pinned on the French Emperor. Among the progressively minded conservatives of his day, this view was by no means unusual. The battles fought by Napoleon appeared initially, even in Germany, in a different light from the horrifying bloodbath of the Revolution. They were not tainted by the stigma of civil war and irrational violence, but appeared almost as if suffused in the light of a higher reason, and served, so it was believed, to promote the dissemination of the ideas of equality and tolerance. It is not wholly without irony, though, that our Almanac author reports that when the call went out for the Great Sanhedrin in Paris, there were some among the Jewish population in France who believed that the Emperor intended 'to send the Jews back to their old homeland on the great mountain of Lebanon, by the river of Egypt and by the sea'. The longer the Napoleonic wars continue, however, the more Hebel's optimism fades. In a short piece omitted from the Almanac of 1811, the *Hausfreund*, who is after all good with figures, calculates matter-of-factly how many hundred thousand men and x-thousand horses Napoleon has got through each year, and how many hundred millions the mustering and equipping of his armies continue to swallow up. In another piece, also not included in the Almanac, he illustrates the madness of warfare in terms of what it takes to build a single one of the ships which are, on the whole, destined before long to be sunk in a naval battle: '1,000 mighty oak trees, as one might say a whole forest; further 200,000 pounds of iron. For the sails it takes 6,500 ells of canvas; the weight of the ropes and rigging is 164,000 pounds, and once they have been coated in tar, as they need to be, they would weigh 200,000 pounds. The total weight of the whole ship amounts to 5 million pounds or 50,000 hundredweight, without the crew and provisions, not counting the powder and lead for the ammunition.' The Almanac author, accustomed to thrift and good housekeeping, is aghast at the idea of such wastefulness, the mere thought of which 'makes his hair stand on end'. In 1814, when the tide has finally turned, he declares his horror at the pointless destruction, under the heading 'World Events' ['Weltbegebenheiten'], in a report on the conflagration in Moscow, at that time the greatest city in the world: 'Four districts of the inner city and thirty suburbs with all the houses, palaces, churches, chapels, taverns, shops, factories, schools and government offices went up in flames. Previously, the city had 400,000 inhabitants and was over twelve leagues across,' writes the *Hausfreund*, and continues, 'If one stood and looked down from a height, as far as the eye could see there was nothing but sky and Moscow. Thereafter, nothing but sky and flames. For hardly had the French occupied the city than the Russians themselves set fire on all sides. A steady wind quickly spread the flames into every quarter of the city. In three days the greater part of the latter was reduced to rubble and ashes, and for anyone passing that way, there was nothing left to see but sky and desolation.' Later on in his report on these epoch-making world events, Hebel reminds his Almanac readers of the order issued in Berlin on the 6th of May 1813, according to which, should the Battle of the Nations go against them, all men under the age of sixty were to arm themselves, all women, children and official persons, surgeons, civil servants and so on to conceal themselves from the enemy, and all livestock and provisions to be disposed of. 'All the fruits of the field, all ships and bridges, all villages and mills are to be burned, all wells blocked up, so that the enemy may nowhere find either abode or succour. Never before,' writes the *Hausfreund*, 'has such a dreadful and drastic measure been taken for the destruction of one's own country.' In our own times we can get a sense of something of the horror which befell the Almanac author as he gazed down into the already gaping maw of history if we remind ourselves how, towards the end of the 1920s, the

27

German *Wehrmacht*, under the direction of Colonel Stülpnagel, drew up a plan for a war of revenge against the French which – as Karl-Heinz Janßen reports, in an article* about the files discovered by the Hamburg historian Carl Dirks in the American National Archives – in a curious mixture of revolutionary idealism *à la* 1813 and hardheaded pragmatism, stipulated that the *Ur*-enemy was to be provoked into invading Germany, there enmeshed in an endless series of partisan battles, and finally defeated by a strategy of scorched earth. To facilitate the action, writes Janßen, special maps of destruction were drawn up expressly for this purpose for the whole area of the Reich, and were called to mind again in 1945 in the final, suicidal weeks of the war. Possibly Hebel already had a sense, in 1812/13, that the fall of Napoleon and the rise of the German peoples signalled the beginning of a downward path which, once embarked upon, would not be easy to halt, and that history, from that point on, would amount to nothing other than the martyrology of mankind. At any rate, I can imagine that the Almanac author felt somewhat ill at ease when, in January 1814, he composed a six-page *Patriotisches Mahnwort* [patriotic exhortation] in which he – otherwise apt to observe matters with a certain detachment – adopts the impassioned martial tones which were everywhere in vogue at the time. 'Behold,' it says there, 'here arises and has already arisen – fully armed – all Germany from the sea to the mountains. All the noble tribes of German blood, the Prussians, the Saxons, the people of Hessen, the Franks, the Bavarians, the Swabians, all who speak and are German, along the length of the Rhine and far away on the

* Cf. *Die Zeit*, 7 March 1997. (Footnote by WGS.)

28

Danube, all are one man, one courage, one *Bund* and one oath: *Deutschland* shall be free from foreign yoke and curse!' Hebel then goes on to describe the protection of the *Heimat* and the rebirth of the nation, the five million muskets, axes, pikes and scythes which shall rise up in Germany, the vagaries of fate, blood sacrifice and sacred sites, and exhorts his cousin, to whom this epistle is addressed as his brother, fellow countryman and German comrade-in-arms, to enlist in the ranks of the defenders of the Fatherland, and thus enter into God's salvation. The chauvinistic registers Hebel draws on here are those of the new nationalist rhetoric, whose resonance, growing ever stronger over the course of the following hundred years, so distracted German society that it would eventually seek to replicate the Napoleonic experiment of the reorganization of Europe under the leadership of another dictator obsessed with the unconditional will to power. In 1966, Jean Dutourd of the Académie Française published a deliberately politically incorrect *essai* about the era 1789–1815, written from the viewpoint of an unreformed monarchist. Entitled *Le Feld-maréchal von Bonaparte*, it starts from the premise that during the pre-1789 monarchic order of Europe, in which the ruling houses were, without exception, all interrelated through marriage and family ties, armed conflicts had as a rule to be kept within limits; and that, while these confrontations served the pursuit of particular territorial or other concrete advantages, they were never governed by one over-arching abstract idea. Only with the invention of revolutionary patriotism, thus Dutourd, did history get caught up in an ever-accelerating maelstrom of destruction. For that reason, Dutourd writes, it would

have been more sensible if the garrison at the Bastille had opened
fire on the insurgents, thus aborting from the outset the transformation – during the Revolution – of a population of honest
and hard-working subjects into a nation of savages, and would
consequently also have prevented the rise of the *parvenu* from
Corsica. The latter, says Dutourd, was indeed possessed of all the
necessary attributes for the model of a successful usurper – ambition, genius, willpower, covetousness, obsession with fame and
order, and a complete and utter lack of sensitivity – but in order
truly to become Emperor of the Western world, 'il lui fallait
tomber dans une société éclatée'.[17] The blood shed in this era
between 1789 and 1815, Dutourd claims, not only changed the
nature of the French themselves, as well as the face of their country; from its smouldering ruins there also arose the new and
terrifying *Deutschland*. In the earlier, innocent, Germania,
Dutourd believes, no philosopher would ever have had the idea
of exclaiming *Allemagne, réveille-toi!* 'Pour la tirer de sa léthargie,
il ne fallait pas moins que les canons de l'empéreur des Français.
Cette Allemagne qui est devenue si formidable au XXe siècle,
c'est bien nous, hélas! qui l'avons faite, qui l'avons tirée du
néant.'[18] Perhaps the violence of the historical currents which
Dutourd discusses in his unorthodox treatise can most readily be
measured if one remembers that they moved the Almanac author
to compose not only his unfortunate patriotic exhortation of
1814, but also an eschatalogical vision unparalleled in German
literature. The scene we must imagine is the Basel road between
Steinen and Brombach at night. The father – *der Ätti* – and his
young son are travelling in the slow oxcart pulled by the faithful

oxen Merz and Laubi —'*Hörsch, wie der Laubi schnuuft?*' ['Listen, how Laubi snorts'] says the boy at one point — and their conversation turns to the transience of earthly existence, of all human endeavour, the houses and villages in which we live, the great cities, Nature in all her greenery, and the whole world. When the boy asks whether their own house, up there on the hill with the lights glinting in its window panes, will meet the same fate as the castle of Rötteln, which is now nothing but a dark and dismal ruin, the father answers:

> *Jo, wegerli, und 's Hus wird alt und wüest;*
> *der Rege wäscht der's wüester alli Nacht,*
> *und d'Sunne bleicht der's schwärzer alli Tag,*
> *und im Vertäfer popperet der Wurm.*
> *Es regnet no dur Bühni ab, es pfift*
> *der Wind dur d'Chlimse. Drüber tuesch du au*
> *no d'Auge zue; es chömme Chindeschind,*
> *und pletze dra. Z'letzt fuults im Fundement,*
> *und 's hilft nüt me. Und wemme nootno gar*
> *zweitusig zehlt, isch alles z'semme g'keit.*

[Yes it's true, and the house is growing old and dirty too; the rain washes it dirtier every night and the sun bleaches it blacker every day and the beetles tick in the wainscots. The rain will come through the loft, the wind will whistle through the cracks. Meantime you will have closed your eyes too and your children's children will come and patch it up. At long last it will get the rot in the foundations and then there'll be no help for it. And by the year two thousand everything will have tumbled down.][19]

A little later in this Alemannic discourse on decay and death, the father comes to speak of the future fate of Basel — 'e schöni, tolli Stadt' ['a fine town, a grand town'], yet it too must fall:

> 's eitue, Chind, es schlacht e mol e Stund,
> goht Basel au ins Grab, und streckt no do
> und dört e Glied zum Boden us, e Joch,
> en alte Turn, e Giebelwand; es wachst
> do Holder druf, do Büechli, Tanne dört,
> und Moos und Farn, und Reiger niste drinn —
> 's isch schad derfür!

[There's nothing for it, son, the hour will strike when even Basel will go down to the grave too, and just poke up a limb here and there out of the ground, a beam, an old tower, a gable; the elder will grow on it, beeches here, firs there, and moss and fern, and herons will nest in it — such a pity!]

The Almanac author, who sometimes in his stories hints that his true home was once a less bigoted Orient, and whom I can easily imagine wandering around in turban and flowing robes among Turks and Jews, includes in this beautiful valedictory image of Basel elements which are distinctly reminiscent of Petra and the other ruined cities of the East, even though the fir trees and elder bushes, the ferns and moss growing on the ruins, are more at home in the Black Forest and the Alps. The peace which has descended on Basel, though, is that of nature untouched by human hand, where abandoned channels and water-meadows are allowed to flood at will, and herons circle overhead. Far more terrifying, though, is the next image that the father evokes, of war and destruction and a world going up in flames, completely in accordance with the apocalyptic doctrine of the end of the world which bourgeois philosophy has suppressed as irreconcilable with the higher principles of rational thought. Since, though, it is precisely the emancipation of the bourgeoisie – of which Hebel was of course a member – which established the economic and philosophical prerequisites for the catastrophes capable of turning whole continents upside down, the terrible fire and lightning blazing through the following lines is not just a reflection of biblical eschatology – with whose metaphorical arsenal the Almanac author and Baden cleric was naturally fully conversant – but also the doom-laden glimmering of a new age which, even as it dreams of humanity's greatest possible happiness, begins to set in train its greatest possible misfortune. Nothing now is left of the consolations of nature which suffuse the earlier image of the ruin of Basel:

> Es goht e Wächter us um Mitternacht,
> e fremde Ma, me weiß nit, wer er isch,
> er funkelt, wie ne Stern, und rüeft: 'Wacht auf!
> Wacht auf, es kommt der Tag!' – Drob rötet si
> der Himmel, und es dundert überal,
> z'erst heimlig, alsg'mach lut, wie sellemol,

wo Anno Sechsenünzgi der Franzos
so uding gschosse het. Der Bode schwankt,
aß d'Chilchtürn guge; d'Glocke schlagen a,
und lüte selber Bettzit wit und breit,
und alles bettet. Drüber chunnt der Tag;
o, b'hüetis Gott, me brucht ke Sunn derzue,
der Himmel stoht im Blitz, und d'Welt im Glast.
Druf gschieht no viel, i ha jez nit der Zit;
Und endli zündet's a, und brennt und brennt,
wo Boden isch, und niemes löscht.

[A watchman will go out at midnight, a foreign chap
nobody knows, he'll glitter like a star and cry, 'Awake!
Behold, the day is come!' and the sky will turn red and
there'll be thunder everywhere, first soft, then loud like
that time in ninety-six when the French bombarded so
fiercely. The ground will shake so that the church towers
will rock, the bells will sound and ring out for the service
by themselves to all and sundry, and everyone will pray.
Then the day will come; O God preserve us, there will
be no need of any sun, the sky will be nothing but lightning
and the world will be all afire. And a lot more will happen
that I've no time for now, and at last it will catch fire and
blaze and blaze, wherever there is any land, and no one to
put it out.]

In its closing passage, Hebel's poem on the transience of the
glories of the world becomes wholly identified with the vision

of the Book of Revelations. In it we hear of a city hidden among
the stars which the boy, if he is good, may eventually enter:

Siehsch nit, wie d'Luft mit schöne Sterne prangt!
's isch jede Stern veglichlige ne Dorf,
und witer obe seig e schöni Stadt,
me sieht si nit vo do, und haltsch di guet,
se chunnsch in so ne Stern, und 's isch der wohl,
und findisch der Ätti dört, wenn's Gottswill isch,
und 's Chüngi selig, d'Muetter. Öbbe fahrsch
au d'Milchstraß uf in die verborgeni Stadt,
und wenn de sitwärts abe luegsch, was siehsch?
e Röttler Schloß! Der Belche stoht vercholt,
der Blauen au, as wie zwee alti Türn,
und zwische drinn isch alles uße brennt,
bis tief in Boden abe. D'Wiese het
ke Wasser meh, 's ish alles öd und schwarz,
und totestill, so wit me luegt − das siehsch,
und seisch di'm Kamerad, wo mitder goht:
'Lueg, dört isch d'Erde gsi, und selle Berg
het Belche gheiße! Nit gar wit dervo
ischWisleth gsi; dört hani au scho glebt,
und Stiere g'wettet, Holz go Basel g'füehrt,
und brochet, Matte g'raust, und Liechtspöh' g'macht,
und g'vätterlet, bis an mi selig End,
und möchte jez nümme hi!'

[Do you see how the sky is splendid with bright stars? Each star is as it might be a village, and farther up perhaps there is a fine town, you can't see it from here, and if you live decent you will go to one of those stars and you'll be happy there, and you'll find your father there, if it is God's will, and poor Bessie, your mother. Perhaps you'll drive up the Milky Way into that hidden town, and if you look down to one side, what'll you see – Rötteln Castle! The Belchen will be charred and the Blauen too, like two old towers, and between the two everything will be burnt out, right into the ground. There won't be any water in the Wiese, everything will be bare and black and deathly quiet, as far as you can see; you'll see that and say to your mate that's with you: 'Look, that's where the earth was, and that mountain was called the Belchen. And not far away was Wieslet; I used to live there and harness my oxen, cart wood to Basel and plough, and drain meadows and make splints for torches, and potter about until my death, and I wouldn't like to go back now!']

The view from the Milky Way back down to the bleak and black-ened ruins of the earth spinning in space could not appear more strange, and yet the childhood we spent on it, and which echoes through the words of the *Hausfreund*, seems scarcely more distant than the day before last.

J'aurais voulu que ce lac eût été l'Océan . . .

On the occasion of a visit
to the Île Saint-Pierre

At the end of September 1965, having moved to the French-speaking part of Switzerland to continue my studies, a few days before the beginning of the semester I took a trip to the nearby Seeland, where, starting from Ins, I climbed up the so-called Schattenrain.[1] It was a hazy sort of day, and I remember how, on reaching the edge of the small wood covering the slope, I paused to look back down at the path I had come by, at the plain stretching away to the north criss-crossed by the straight lines of canals, with the hills shrouded in mist beyond; and how, when I emerged once more into the fields above the village of Lüscherz, I saw spread out below me the Lac de Bienne, and sat there for an hour or more lost in thought at the sight, resolving that at the earliest opportunity I would cross over to the island in the lake which, on that autumn day, was flooded with a trembling pale light. As so often happens in life, however, it took another thirty-one years before this plan could be realized and I was finally able, in the early summer of 1996, in the company of an exceedingly obliging host who lived high above the steep shores of the lake and who habitually wore a kind of captain's cap, smoked Indian *bidis* and seldom spoke,[2] to make the journey across the lake from the city of Bienne to the island of Saint-Pierre, formed during the last ice age by the retreating Rhône glacier into the shape of a whale's back — or so it is generally said. The ship which took us

along the edge of the Jura massif where it plunges steeply into the lake was called the *Ville de Fribourg*. Among the other passengers on board were the gaudily attired members of a male-voice choir, who several times during the short crossing struck up from the stern a chorus of 'Là-haut sur la montagne, Les jours s'en vont' or another such Swiss refrain, with the sole intention, or so it seemed to me, of reminding me, with the curiously strained, guttural notes their ensemble produced, of how far I had come meanwhile from my place of origin.

Apart from a single farmstead, there is now only one dwelling on the Île Saint-Pierre — an island with a circumference of some two miles — and that is a former Cluniac monastery which now houses a hotel and restaurant run by Blausee AG. After walking there from the landing stage, I sat for a while drinking coffee with my companion in the shady trellised courtyard, until it was time for him to take his leave and I watched from the gate as he made his way slowly down the white path, just like a sailor who, I thought to myself, after years of sailing the high seas finds himself washed up on the unfamiliar mainland once more. The room I took at the hotel looked out on the south side of the building, directly adjacent to the two rooms which Jean-Jacques Rousseau occupied when, in September 1765, exactly 200 years before my first sight of the island from the top of the Schattenrain, he found refuge here, at least until the Berne *Petit Conseil* drove him out from even this last outpost of his native land. 'By Saturday next,' as an edict sent to the *Bailli* in Nidau stated, 'the said M. Rousseau is to remove himself from your Excellencies' territories and shall not be permitted to return save under pain of the severest penalty.' In the decades after Rousseau's death, when his fame had spread throughout Europe and beyond, an endless procession of illustrious personages visited the island to see for themselves the place in which the philosopher, novelist, autobiographer and inventor of the bourgeois cult of romantic sensibility was for a brief period — as he claims in the fifth *Promenade* in the *Reveries of*

41

the Solitary Walker – happier than in any other place. The adventurer and confidence trickster Cagliostro, the French *conseiller du Parlement* Desjobert, the English statesman Thomas Pitt, diverse kings of Prussia, Sweden and Bavaria all came to the island, not least among them the former Empress Joséphine. Early in the morning of the 30th of September 1810, hours before the arrival of the most beautiful woman of her day, a crowd a thousand strong was already waiting by the shore, and on the lake itself the ships and boats garlanded with flowers and flags thronged together in such numbers that the water could scarcely be seen. And when, twenty years later, the Poles arrived in Switzerland after the violent suppression of their uprising, the island on more than one occasion served as a meeting place where the refugees – for many a source of admiration – and the liberals who sympathized with their cause organized ceremonies to commemorate those who had fallen in the fight for freedom. On one such occasion in 1833, as Werner Henzi recalls in his prospectus of the Rousseau island, an enthusiastic crowd surrounded an altar set up between two chestnut trees, covered in black cloth, on which the book of the Rights of Man lay shrouded in black crêpe while the nearby trees were decorated with the Lithuanian coat of arms and the White Eagle, emblem of the ancient Polish nation. Throughout the nineteenth century, too, other, private individuals included Rousseau's island on their itineraries, sensitive and cultivated readers such as, for example, the young Englishwoman Caroline Stanley, who visited the Lac de Bienne in the summer of 1820 and painted this view of the Île Saint-Pierre – along with the Grindelwald glacier and other wonders of the Swiss landscape – in her watercolour album, which I came upon recently in an antiquarian bookshop in Zurich. A number of these visitors, too, carved their initials or the date of their visits with a penknife on to the door-jambs and window-seat of the Rousseau room, and as one runs a finger along these grooves in the wood, one wishes one could know who they were and what has become of them.

In the course of our own century, now nearing its end, this Rousseau mania has gradually abated. At any rate, in the few days I spent on the island – during which time I passed not a few hours sitting by the window in the Rousseau room – among the tourists who come over to the island on a day trip for a stroll or a bite to eat, only two strayed into this room with its sparse furnishings – a settee, a bed, a table and a chair – and even those two, evidently disappointed at how little there was to see, soon left again. Not one of them bent down to look at the glass display case to try to decipher Rousseau's handwriting, nor noticed the way that the bleached deal floorboards, almost two feet wide, are so worn down in the middle of the room as to form a shallow depression, nor that in places the knots in the wood protrude by almost an inch. No one ran a hand over the stone basin worn smooth by age in the antechamber, or noticed the smell of soot which still lingers in the fireplace, nor paused to look out of the window with its view across the orchard and a meadow to the island's southern shore. For me, though, as I sat in Rousseau's room, it was as if I had been transported back to an earlier age, an illusion I could indulge in all the more readily inasmuch as the island still retained that same quality of silence, undisturbed by

43

even the most distant sound of a motor vehicle, as was still to be found everywhere in the world a century or two ago. Towards evening, especially, when the day-trippers had returned home, the island was immersed in a stillness such as is scarcely now to be found anywhere in the orbit of our civilized world, and where nothing moved, save perhaps the leaves of the mighty poplars in the breezes which sometimes stirred along the edge of the lake. The paths strewn with a fine limestone gravel grew ever brighter as I walked along them in the gathering dusk, past fenced-in meadows, past a pale motionless field of oats, a vineyard, and a vintner's hut, up to the terrace at the edge of the beech wood already black with night, from where I watched the lights go on one after another on the opposite shore. The darkness seemed to rise out of the lake, and for a moment as I stood there gazing down into it, an image arose in my mind which somewhat resembled a colour plate in an old natural history book and which – though more precise and more attractive by far than any such coloured print – revealed numerous fish of the lake as they hung sleeping in the deep currents between the dark walls of water, above and behind each other, larger and smaller ones, roach and rudd, bleaks and barbels, char and trout, dace and minnows, catfish, zander and pike and tench and graylings and crucian carp.

When Rousseau fled to the Île Saint-Pierre in the autumn of 1765, he was already on the verge of utter physical and mental exhaustion. Between 1751 and 1761, in his fifth decade and in ever more precarious health, he had, first in Paris and then in the Ermitage at Montmorency, committed to paper thousands upon thousands of pages. The *Discourse on the Sciences and the Arts*, which

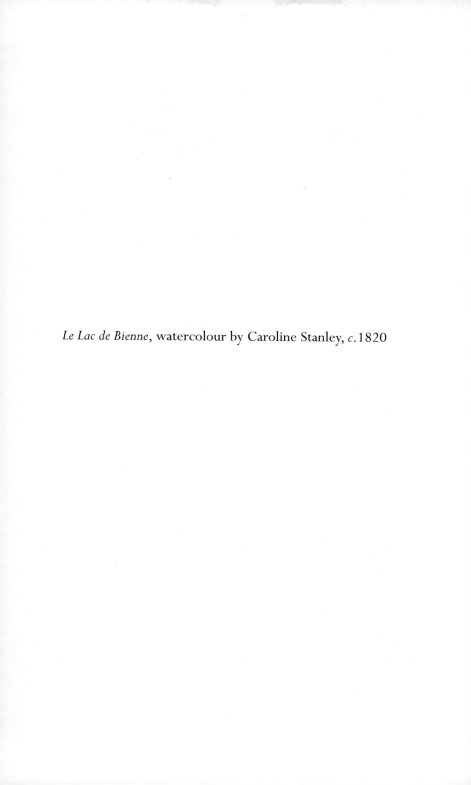

Le Lac de Bienne, watercolour by Caroline Stanley, c.1820

earned him the prize of the Académie de Dijon, the treatise *On the Origin and Basis of Inequality among Men*, the opera *Le Devin du village*, the letters on French music and on Providence, to Voltaire and to D'Alembert, the fairytale *La Reine fantasque*, the novel *La Nouvelle Héloïse*; *Émile*, and *The Social Contract* — all this and more was written during this period alongside the extremely copious correspondence which Rousseau always maintained. When one considers the extent and diversity of this creative output, one can only assume that Rousseau must have spent the entire time hunched over his desk in an attempt to capture, in endless sequences of lines and letters, the thoughts and feelings incessantly welling up within him. Scarcely had he reached the apogee of literary fame for his passionate epistolary novel proclaiming the natural rights of lovers, than the state of nervous exhaustion resulting from this manic productivity was further exacerbated when *Émile* and the *Social Contract* were banned and confiscated by the *parlement* in Paris, thus making of the celebrated author an outcast, ostracized and banished from France on pain of arrest. Nor does Rousseau fare any better in his native city of Geneva. Here too he is condemned as a godless and seditious person, and his writings consigned to the flames. Looking back on this time when fate turned against him, Rousseau writes in 1770, at the beginning of the last book of his *Confessions*: 'Here commences the work of darkness, in which, for eight years past, I have been entombed, without ever having been able, in spite of all my efforts, to penetrate its frightful obscurity. In the abyss of misfortune in which I am submerged, I feel the . . . blows which are directed against me. I perceive their immediate instrument, but

I cannot see either the hand which guides them or the means which it employs. Shame and misfortune fall upon me as if of themselves, and unawares.' A temporary refuge is vouchsafed him only when he reaches Neuchâtel, a territory under Prussian rule and governed by Lord Marischal George Keith, where Rousseau's admirer, Madame Boy de la Tour, places at his disposal a vacant farmhouse in Môtiers, in the remote Val de Travers. The first winter Rousseau passes there is one of the coldest of the century. The first snows fall in October. Despite his chronic abdominal complaints and the various other illnesses and ailments which plague him, from this inhospitable exile Rousseau defends himself as best he can against the incessant allegations which the Geneva Council and the clergy of Neuchâtel lay at his door. From time to time the darkness appears to lift a little. Rousseau pays calls on his protector, Lord Keith, whose ménage includes the Kalmuck Stéfan, the negro Motcho, Ibrahim the Tartar and Ermentulla, a Muslim woman from Armenia. In this tolerant environment the persecuted philosopher, who at this period has already taken to wearing his infamous Armenian garb, a kind of kaftan and fur bonnet, appears not in the least incongruous. Moreover, he is at pains to accommodate himself with Georges de Montmollin, the pastor in Môtiers, going to mass and communion; he sits in front of the house in the sun occupying himself with the weaving of silk ribbons, and goes botanizing along the valley and in the alpine pastures. 'Il me semble,' he writes later in the *Rêveries*, 'que sous les ombrages d'une forêt je suis oublié, libre et paisible comme si je n'avais plus d'ennemis.'[3] The enemies, meanwhile, were not idle. Rousseau sees himself obliged to write a letter in his own defence to the Archbishop of Paris, and a year later the pamphlet *Lettres de la montagne*, in which he demonstrates how the Geneva Council's proceedings against him offend against both the constitution of that Republic and its liberal traditions. Voltaire, orchestrating the campaign against Rousseau from behind the scenes in an unholy alliance with the self-righteous representatives of the *classe vénérable*, responded to this missive with a pamphlet entitled *Le Sentiment des citoyens*, in which, having failed to send Rousseau to the scaffold, he attempts to denounce him as a charlatan and a blasphemous liar. He does this not under his own name but anonymously, in the style of a fanatical Calvinist minister. Full of shame and sorrow – thus the pamphlet – one is forced to the conclusion that in Rousseau, one is dealing with a man who still bears the deadly marks of his debauchery, and in the costume of a travelling showman drags with him from town to town and mountain top to mountain top the wretched woman whose mother he sent to an early grave and whose children he abandoned at the door of the foundlings' home, thereby not only forswearing any natural feeling but at the same time divesting himself of all honour and religion. It is not immediately clear why Voltaire, who in the course of his career did not otherwise notably distinguish himself as a defender of the true faith, should have taken up the cause against Rousseau with such vehemence, nor why he should have hounded him so relentlessly and with such venom. The only possible explanation seems to be that he was unable to come to terms with his own fame being eclipsed by the light of this new star in the literary firmament. Few things are as immutable as the vindictiveness with which writers talk about their literary colleagues behind their backs. But however such matters may have stood at the time, Voltaire's public invective and his scheming behind the scenes finally resulted in Rousseau's having to leave the Val de Travers. When the Marquise de Verdelin visited him in Môtiers in early September 1765 and attended a Sunday service there, Montmollin, who for a while at least had been favourably disposed towards Rousseau, but had increasingly come under the influence of his colleagues from Neuchâtel and Geneva, delivered a sermon on the verse in Proverbs 15 which states that the participation of the wicked in the sacrifice of the Lord is an abomination. Not even the simplest soul among the faithful present that day in the church at Môtiers could have been in any doubt as to who this inflammatory sermon was aimed at. It is scarcely surprising, then, that henceforth whenever Rousseau appeared on the street he was sworn at and mobbed by the angry villagers, and that the same night stones were hurled at the gallery and thrown through the windows of his house. Rousseau writes later, in the *Confessions*, that at the time in the Val de Travers he was treated like a rabid wolf and that, passing one of the scattered cottages, he would sometimes hear one of the peasants call out, 'Fetch me my gun so that I can take a shot at him.'

Compared with these dark days, the Île Saint-Pierre must truly have appeared to Rousseau, when he arrived there on the 9th of September, as a paradise in miniature in which he might believe he could collect himself in a stillness, as he writes at the beginning of the Fifth Walk, interrupted only by the cry of the eagle, the song of an occasional bird, and the rushing of the mountain streams. During his stay on the island Rousseau was provided for

by the steward Gabriel Engel and his wife Salome, who managed
the farmstead with a few servants, and were later reprimanded
by the Berne Council for having unquestioningly taken in the
refugee without further ado. None the less, Rousseau was hardly
as solitary on the island in September and October 1765 as the
Fifth Walk would have us believe. As in Môtiers, here too he was
subject to the attentions of a steady stream of visitors, from whom
he frequently found himself obliged to escape via the trapdoor

which is still to be seen in his room to this day. Nor were the months
of the harvest, during which large numbers of people from Bienne
and its surroundings were employed on the island, quite such a
peaceful time as Rousseau might in retrospect believe. Nevertheless we can easily understand how, after all he had had to endure
in Môtiers, he could believe that he could easily spend two years,
two centuries or all of eternity on the island in the care of the

Engels. That at least is almost exactly how I felt when, returning at dusk from my walk on the first evening of my stay, I sat alone in the dining room of the hotel. Outside, night had fallen, and inside I was lapped in the warm glow of a lamp and looked after most attentively by the *patron* himself, who came over to my table from time to time to see whether everything was in order and whether there was anything further I desired. This *patron*, one Herr Regli, who that evening was wearing an apricot-coloured suit and appeared almost to glide through the rooms, seemed to me the very model of courtesy and consideration, and my admiration for him was complete when I later heard him say on the telephone, as he sat in his little office, yes, yes, of course he was still there, *vous me connaissez, toujours fidèle au poste*.

Nor was there any let-up for Rousseau, during his stay on the island, in the daily business of writing, even if he claimed, in the fifth *Promenade*, to have sought to extricate himself from it by any means possible. Apart from his ceaseless correspondence, during these weeks he was occupied with the editing of his *Projet de constitution pour la Corse*, not published until almost one hundred years later, which he wrote down in two small notebooks today

preserved in the Library of Geneva. The casual remark Rousseau made in the *Social Contract*, that it is time that a wise man by means of a draft constitution showed the Corsican people – then engaged in their struggle for independence from Genoese rule – how they might set about legislating their affairs of state, had led Captain Mathieu Buttafoco to pay a visit to Môtiers to ask the philosopher to take this role upon himself. There was in Europe at the time a great deal of support for the Corsicans' protest against foreign rule, and the Corsican general Pascal Paoli, the father of the fatherland, represented a lodestar for all those who longed to see a better regime. We encounter him in Hölderlin as well as in Hebel's Alemannic poems, where a beggar sitting by the side of the road relates: 'I ha in schwarzer Wetternacht / vor Laudons Zelt und Fahne gwacht / I bi bim Paschal Paoli / in Korsika Draguner gsi' ['In darkest night, in deepest dark / I watched by Laudon's tent and flag / I served with Pascal Paoli / with Corsican dragoons did I'].[4] In Rousseau's imagination, too, the idea of Corsica takes on legendary traits from the beginning; he believed he had a premonition that 'un jour cette petite île étonnera l'Europe',[5] even if he could not have known in what terrifying manner this prophecy was to be fulfilled within the next fifty years. He saw, in Corsica, the potential for putting into practice an order in which the evils of the society in which he felt himself trapped could be avoided. His aversion to urban civilization motivated him to suggest the Corsicans adopt agriculture as the only possible basis for a truly good and free life. All forms of hierarchy were to be avoided by means of a legal system administered through rural communities and based on the principle of equality, as in the cantons of central Switzerland. Above and beyond this Rousseau went so far as to recommend (at the time when Pascal Paoli was busy establishing his own mint in Corte) that the Corsicans abolish monetary economy in favour of a system of bartering. The whole Corsica project outlined on the Île Saint-Pierre is thus a utopian dream in which bourgeois society, increasingly determined by the manufacture of goods and the accumulation of private wealth, is promised a return to more innocent times. Neither Rousseau, nor those who came after him, were ever able to resolve the inherent contradiction between this nostalgic utopia and the inexorable march of progress towards the brink of the abyss. The gap between our longings and our rational strategy for living is clearly illustrated by the fact that Rousseau, who at that time needed nothing more urgently than a safe haven, could not bring himself to move to Corsica. For all that the *Gazette de Berne* had already announced that he would be taking up the position of Governor on the Mediterranean island, if truth be told, having acquired his reputation in the salons of the eminent society of the day, he had no inclination to return to what, from his perspective, appeared as a pre-civilized world, in which, as he notes in the *Confessions*, the most basic comforts would be lacking. He is positively horrified at the prospect of crossing the Alps and having to transport with him his entire household effects – 'linge, habits, vaisselle, batterie de cuisine, papier, livres,' he writes, 'il fallait tout porter avec soi'.[6] The place where he had been offered accommodation and a living was Vescovato, a small town huddled high up on one of the steep east-facing slopes of the Castagniccia. In the eighteenth century it was a place of some importance, and the Filippini house which would have been at his disposal was by no means as primitive as perhaps he feared. I visited it a few months after I had been to the Île Saint-Pierre. From the first-floor windows one looks down into a steep gorge which even at the end of summer is alive with the sound of water. Further away, one perceives a shimmering blue haze in which it is impossible to distinguish the sea from the sky rising above it. The town is surrounded by cultivated terraces, abandoned now, but in which at that time fruit trees flourished, oranges and apricots and various fruits of the field. In the surrounding area, covering the slopes of the hills, were groves of sweet chestnuts in whose dappled shade Rousseau could have taken the air with his dog at his side. Who can say whether, if he had spent the rest of his life there, far removed from the hubbub of literary business and hypocrisy, he might yet have retained that sense of sanity and proportion which later at times threatened to desert him altogether.

Although Rousseau was by no means idle as an author in the few weeks he spent on the Île Saint-Pierre, in retrospect he none the less came to see this time as an attempt to free himself from the exigencies of literary production. He talks of how he longs now for something other than literary renown, the scent of which, as he says, revolted him from the very moment he first got a whiff of it. The *dégoût* Rousseau now felt with regard to literature was not merely an intermittent emotional reaction but something that for him always went hand in hand with the act of writing. In accordance with his doctrine of the formerly unspoiled state of Nature, he saw the man who reflects as a depraved animal perverted from its natural state, and reflection as a degraded form of mental energy. No one, in the era when the bourgeoisie was proclaiming, with enormous philosophical and literary effort, its entitlement to emancipation, recognized the pathological aspect of thought as acutely as Rousseau, who himself wished for nothing more than to be able to halt the wheels ceaselessly turning within his head. If he nevertheless persevered with writing, then only, as Jean Starobinski notes, in order to hasten the moment when the pen would fall from his hand and the essential things would be said in the *silent* embrace of reconciliation and return.[7] Less heroically, but certainly no less correctly, one could also see writing as a continually self-perpetuating compulsive act, evidence that, of all individuals afflicted by the disease of thought, the writer is perhaps the most incurable. The copying out of musical notation, which Rousseau was constrained to undertake in his earlier years and at the last in Paris, was for him one of the few means of keeping at bay the thoughts constantly brewing in his head like storm clouds. How difficult it is in general to bring the machinery of thought to a standstill is shown by Rousseau's description of his apparently so happy days on the island in the Lac de Bienne. He has, as he writes in the Fifth Walk, deliberately forsworn the burden of work, and his greatest joy has been to leave his books safely shut away and to have neither ink nor paper to hand. However, since the leisure time thus freed up must be put to some use, Rousseau devotes himself to the study of botany, whose basic principles he had acquired in Môtiers on excursions with Jean Antoine d'Ivernois. 'I set out to compose,' writes Rousseau in the Fifth Walk, 'a Flora

Petrinsularis and to describe every single plant on the island in enough detail to keep me busy for the rest of my days. They say a German once wrote a book about a lemon-peel; I could have written one about every grass in the meadows, every moss in the woods, every lichen covering the rocks – and I did not want to leave even one blade of grass or atom of vegetation without a full and detailed description. In accordance with this noble plan, every morning after breakfast I would set out with a magnifying glass in my hand and my *Systemae Naturae* under my arm to study one particular section of the island, which I had divided for this purpose into small squares, intending to visit them all one after another in every season.' The central motif of this passage is not so much the impartial insight into the indigenous plants of the island as that of ordering, classification and the creation of a perfect system. Thus this apparently innocent occupation – the deliberate resolve no longer to think and merely to look at nature – becomes, for the writer plagued by the chronic need to think and work, a demanding rationalistic project involving the compiling of lists, indices and catalogues, along with the precise description of, for example, the long stamens of self-heal,[8] the springiness of those of nettle and of wall-pellitory, and the sudden bursting of the seed capsules of balsam and of beech.[9] None the less, the leaves of the small *herbaria* which Rousseau later compiled for Madelon and Julie de la Tour and other young ladies take on the aspect of an innocent *bricolage* in comparison with the self-destructive business of writing to which he usually submitted himself. A faint aura of unconscious beauty still hovers over these flower collections, in which lichens, sprigs of veronica, lilies-of-

the-valley and autumn crocuses have survived, pressed and a little faded, from the eighteenth century. They can still be admired today in the Musée Carnavalet and the Musée des Arts Décoratifs. The *herbarium* Rousseau compiled for himself, meanwhile — eleven quarto volumes — was, up to the Second World War, preserved in the Botanical Museum in Berlin, until, like so much and so many in that city, it went up in flames one night during one of the nocturnal bombing raids.

Rousseau is only able to experience the true contrast to the employment which even botanizing represents when, on fine days, he rows far out on the calm waters of the lake. 'There, stretching out full-length in the boat,' we read in the chapter on the island, 'and turning my eyes skyward, I let myself float and drift wherever the water took me, often for several hours on end.' The clarity of the sky arching over him out there on the lake is reminiscent of the description of the mountains of the Valais

at the beginning of *La Nouvelle Héloïse* as a landscape freed from
the veils of lower, denser atmosphere, which has something of a
magical, transcendental quality about it and in which one forgets
everything, even oneself, and no longer knows where one is.
'The moment of utmost clarity of the landscape,' writes Jean
Starobinski, who has studied the theme of transparency in Rousseau, 'is at one and the same time the moment at which
individual existence dissolves at its limits and is dreamily transformed into thin air.' To become totally transparent was, according
to Starobinski, the greatest ambition of the inventor of modern
autobiography. The symbol of this ambition is the crystal, for it
is impossible to tell, Starobinski states, whether it is 'a body in
its purest state or, by contrast, a petrified soul'. Starobinski points
out in this context, poised between alchemy and metaphysics,
that Rousseau, in his *Institutions chimiques*, devotes a great deal
of attention to the process of vitrification, quoting a passage in
which Rousseau discusses the author of a volume published in
1669 entitled *Physica subterranea*, one Johann Joachim Becher,[10]
who derives his vitreous earth not merely from the realm of
minerals but also from the ashes of plants and animals. 'He assures
us,' Rousseau writes of Becher, 'that they contain an easily fusi-
ble, vitrifiable earth from which it is possible to make vases
superior to the finest porcelain. Using procedures that he keeps
shrouded in much mystery, he has carried out experiments that
have convinced him that man, like all animals, is glass and can
return to glass. This leads him to the most entertaining reflections
on the trouble the ancients took to burn or embalm the dead,
and on ways in which one might preserve the ashes of one's

ancestors by means of a few hours' work, replacing hideous and disgusting cadavers with clean, shining vases of beautiful, transparent glass, tinted not with the characteristic green of glass made from plants but with a milky white colour heightened by a slight tinge of narcissus.' This conjecture about the metamorphosis of the body into a pure substance, as it were freed from the ephemerality of existence – which Rousseau might well have seen as a metaphor for true artistic production – is, as Starobinski writes, in the final phase of his thought transformed into its 'negative counterpart: pulverization, which kills the light and reduces human society to a dark, indistinguishable and impenetrable mass. No exchange is possible between opposites; Jean-Jacques' transparency is solidified, the dark night outside him congealed. The veil, too, has changed: no longer thin and fluttering, it has descended to enclose the world it once concealed in a web of darkness.'

A dozen years filled with fear and panic await Rousseau after his departure from the Île Saint-Pierre on the 25th of October. He spends a few days in Bienne, which is under the jurisdiction of the Prince Bishop of Basel and where some of the citizens hope to be able to secure him the right to remain, at least for the winter. He spends the first night in the Croix Blanche, and then finds quarters with Masel, a wigmaker of ill-repute, in a room overlooking a stinking tanning pit. Nor are the other signs any more auspicious. Influenced by Berne, which in reality calls the tune in Bienne, several members of the *Magistrat* [municipal council] declare themselves opposed to offering asylum to the stateless refugee. On the 29th, therefore, Rousseau moves on again. From

Basel he writes to Thérèse La Vasseur, the woman who has looked after him for twenty years and the mother of his five long-lost children, saying he is feverish, with a sore throat and sick at heart. His sole consolation is his dog Sultan, who has run for thirty miles ahead of the carriage like a courier and who now, Rousseau continues, is lying asleep on my coat under the table as I write. On the 31st of October, Rousseau leaves Basel, and Switzerland – 'cette terre homicide' as it says on the last page of his autobiography – for good. He is now resolved to take up the offer of asylum in England. The passport issued to him allows him to travel through France, breaking the journey at Strasbourg and Paris, where the world and his wife come to marvel at him and such Rousseau-hysteria prevails that David Hume, who has made use of his ambassadorial influence to intercede in England on Rousseau's behalf, writes to Hugh Blair that he would venture to raise by subscription the sum of £50,000 (an enormous sum in those days) in the French capital in under two weeks, if only Rousseau would allow it. He is such an object of fascination in society (writes Hume) that his housekeeper, La Vasseur, who after all is merely an uneducated woman, is more talked about than the Princess of Monaco or the Countess Egmont. 'His very dog, who is no better than a coly,' Hume adds, 'has a name and reputation in the world.'[11] At the beginning of January 1766 Rousseau travels to England. There, alone in a foreign country, he is increasingly at the mercy of the latent paranoia to which he has always been prone and which, in exile, has become acute. His mood oscillates between despondency and exhilaration. A certain J. Craddock relates in his *Literary and Miscellaneous Memoirs*, published in London in 1828, that Rousseau, despite knowing scarcely any English, on a visit to a theatrical production to which he was invited by Garrick was so overcome with weeping at the tragedy performed that evening, and so transported with laughter at the comedy which followed, that he was quite beside himself, 'and that Mrs Garrick had to hold the skirt of his caftan to prevent his falling out of the box'.[12] Hume had the opportunity to observe these mood-swings for himself when Rousseau came to confide in him about his suspicions and walked darkly up and down in his room for an hour without saying a word, only then suddenly to sit upon his lap, cover his face with kisses and assure him, with tears in his eyes, of his eternal friendship and gratitude. After this it was not long until he came to see Hume, too, as one of the most insidious among the conspirators plotting to deprive him of both his honour and his livelihood. The silent exchange of glances, which in *La Nouvelle Héloïse* indicate the harmony of souls, he now perceives as a threat. Constantly impelled by his fear in a hostile environment to investigate the slightest nuance, any minute irregularity he discovers in the behaviour of a given interlocutor is taken as evidence that the latter is involved in the conspiracy being plotted against him. 'For Jean-Jacques,' Jean Starobinski writes, 'to live amid persecution is to feel caught in a web of interlocking signs.' Every now and then the states of anxiety abate a little. In Wootton in Derbyshire, where he found refuge in a country house belonging to Richard Davenport, a noble elderly gentleman whose acquaintance he had made at a social gathering in London, he enjoyed a brief period of respite, taking up his botanical studies again and writing some of the most lyrical pages of his *Confessions*.

However – not least because Davenport himself was not present in the house to intervene in the misunderstandings which flared up here too – once again everything soon turned sour. Thérèse fell out with the servants, who did not take kindly to being ordered about by this upstart Frenchwoman, and things came to a head in the spring when Davenport's housekeeper set down before the two guests a soup strewn with cinders and ash. Rousseau grows more and more convinced that his every action, and every change in his circumstances, through no fault of his own gives rise to consequences and chains of events beyond his control, making him a prisoner of his enemies conspiring everywhere against him. After leaving Wootton at the beginning of May 1767 in order to return to France, he writes from Spalding in Lincolnshire – a godforsaken place set among endless fields of cabbage and beet – to Lord Chancellor Camden, asking him to place an escort at his disposal so that he may be sure of reaching Dover safely and without undue delay. For three years after his return to France, Rousseau lives with Thérèse – often under an assumed name – in remote country seats of the nobility such as Château Trye in Normandy, or in small towns like Bourgoin or Monquin far away in the South, always with the shadow of outlawry hanging over him. When, in 1770, on condition of not publishing anything on political or religious questions, he receives permission to reside in the capital, attempting to eke out a living there by copying out sheet music, the morbid universe surrounding him can no longer be dispelled. 'The children's grimaces,' Starobinski writes, 'the price of peas in Les Halles, the small shops in the rue Plâtrière – all appeared to be evidence of the same conspiracy.' This

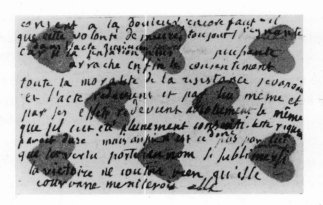

notwithstanding, Rousseau does still succeed in accomplishing a considerable amount. He finishes the *Confessions* and reads from them in various salons in sessions lasting up to seventeen (!) hours, to some extent anticipating Franz Kafka's desire to be allowed to

read aloud, to an audience condemned to listen, the whole of Stendhal's *Éducation sentimentale* at one sitting. There follow a few more treatises, on botany and on the government of Poland, as well as the so-called *Dialogues*, in which Rousseau appears as the judge of Jean-Jacques. In his last two years while out walking he makes notes, on playing cards, for the *Rêveries d'un promeneur solitaire*, which he completes in April 1780. After that he leaves Paris and moves into a small house in the park at Ermenonville which the Marquis de Girardin has placed at his disposal. He lives there for five more weeks in early summer. He rises at dawn, goes for walks, leaning on his cane, in the beautiful surroundings, collects leaves and flowers and sometimes takes a boat out on to the lake. On the 2nd of July – he is sixty-six years old – he comes back from one of his walks with a terrible headache. Thérèse helps him into a chair. Felled by a stroke, he collapses on to the floor and, after a few convulsions, dies. Two days later he is buried at Ermenonville on the Isle of Poplars. In the years which follow, the Marquis

transforms his estate into a *parc du souvenir*. He has a classical monument erected, the Swiss chalet is completed, a Temple of Philosophy is constructed with an altar dedicated to reverie. Even the cabin in front of which Rousseau would often sit on a bench, gazing out over the peaceful landscape, is carefully preserved. The park has become a site of pilgrimage, and more than one lady sinks down before the grave on the island, pressing her bosom against the cold stone beneath which Rousseau's earthly remains rest, until, that is, on the 9th of October 1794 they are transferred to the Panthéon. On this memorable day, a group of musicians performed excerpts from the opera *Le Devin du village*; the oak coffin, triple-lined with lead and further clad with an outer lead covering, was raised from the earth and taken to Paris in a grand and solemn *cortège*. In all the villages along the route the people

lined the streets calling, 'Vive la République! Vive la mémoire de Jean-Jacques Rousseau!' On the evening of the 10th of October the procession arrived at the Tuileries, where a huge crowd was waiting with flaming torches. The coffin, covered by a wooden framework painted with the symbols of the Revolution, was placed on a bier surrounded by a semicircle of willows. The main part of the ceremony took place the following morning, when the funeral procession continued on its way to the Panthéon, led by a captain of the United States Navy bearing the banner of the stars and stripes, and followed by two standard bearers carrying the *tricolore* and the colours of the Republic of Geneva.

Why I grieve
I do not know[1]

A memento of Mörike

When Eduard Mörike arrived in Tübingen to begin his studies at the *Stift* in 1822, the times had already changed. The previous year, the Emperor who had turned the world upside down all over Europe had died rather a miserable death on a rocky outcrop in the desolate wastes of the South Atlantic, and his precursor, the trailblazer with the red Phrygian cap, had also long since vanished from the stage of history. Now the firebrand of the Revolution is only evoked to give a fright to little children. Through their startled eyes we see it flare up one last time outside the window, see it once more burst in at the gate, watch the flames rise from the roof beams and our house collapse in ruins. At the end of this terrible recollection, though, we learn that all that was a very long time ago, and the fire-raiser among us no longer:

> *Nach der Zeit ein Müller fand*
> *Ein Gerippe samt der Mützen*
> *Aufrecht an der Kellerwand*
> *Auf der beinern Mähre sitzen*
> *Feuerreiter, wie so kühle*
> *Reitest du in deinem Grab!*

Husch! Da fällts in Asche ab.
Ruhe wohl,
Ruhe wohl
Drunten in der Mühle!

[Time passed – and a miller found
The rider's skeleton, cap and all,
Leaning on the cellar wall
Still upon his bony mare.
    Fire rider, oh, how coldly,
    You ride to your grave, so boldly!
    Whoosh, to ashes all does fall –
    Rest in peace,
    Rest in peace,
    Below there in the mill!][2]

If, for the young Mörike, the terrors of the Revolution have already receded into a legendary and distant past, the closing acts of the Napoleonic era – the battles of Leipzig and Waterloo, which as a child he must have heard a great deal about – surely formed part of his own memories; and part of the dawning consciousness of his generation was shaped by the hopes for the sovereignty of the people which liberation from French rule was supposed to bring about. The 'wild poet' Waiblinger,[3] whom Mörike met in 1821 and whose writings for a long time continued to hold fast to the revolutionary ideal, is the most apt witness to this. Despite the heavy hand with which the states of the Holy Alliance[4] had been governed for almost a decade, the dream of a national uprising was not yet dead. The clearly drawn lines of 1812 had, however, long since become blurred. Increasingly, visions of the future were becoming less and less clear-cut, and in the minds of the occupants of the Tübingen *Stift,* too, were becoming refracted into that *Ur*-German blend of revolutionary patriotism and bourgeois circumspection, romantic imagination and double-entry book-keeping, political zeal and poetical effusiveness, in which the progressive elements can scarcely any longer be distinguished from the reactionary. 'On the one hand, there was great enthusiasm, with the likes of Byron, Waiblinger and Wilhelm Müller . . . for the Greek Wars of Independence against the Turks, and on the other hand a yearning for the contentment of peace, hearth and home,' writes Holthusen in his monograph on Mörike, in this context also recalling the well-known pen-and-ink drawing by Rudolf Lohbauer showing the artist and his friends 'drinking and smoking in a Tübingen summerhouse which he had furnished as a kind of *buen retiro*'. In this picture, which gives a clear idea of the way the atmosphere of those years oscillated between the impulses of political awakening and retreat from the world, we see, gathered together in the lamplight, five young men dressed in the kind of fanciful costume fashionable at the time as a gesture of rebellion against authority; part olde-worlde German, part modishly rakish: open-necked shirts with wide flowing sleeves, Renaissance berets and suchlike extravagant headgear, sideburns and unkempt locks and those strange small steel-rimmed spectacles which have clearly been the hallmark of the conspiratorial intelligentsia since time immemorial. It is not immediately apparent whether this subversive style, which was

all the rage at the time, was actually an expression of militant liberalism or whether it was mere play-acting and fancy-dress, but one would not be far wrong in assuming that the revolutionary impulse of the Wars of Independence was, from 1820 onwards, beginning to dissolve in a fug of tobacco smoke and *Biergarten* bravado. For almost the whole of the nineteenth century, indeed, one could say that the *Stammtisch* took the place of parliament in Germany. Perhaps this is why, at barely eighteen, Mörike already detects the false notes in the enthusiastic eulogies held by the would-be avant-garde in praise of Kotzebue's murderer, Sand.[5] Admittedly Mörike was, from the outset, even more inclined to resignation than most. In this he is a true representative of a generation which, still just touched by the breath of a heroic age, is preparing to enter upon the becalmed waters of the Biedermeier age, in which bourgeois domesticity takes precedence over public life, and the garden fence becomes the boundary of a life *en famille* which conceives of itself as a universe in its own right.

The calm of the domestic interior and the projection of an image of peaceable domesticity on to the surrounding landscape is one of the recurring motifs of Biedermeier painting. A sparsely furnished study, pale-green walls, scrubbed floors of bleached pine, children playing table skittles, a parrot or parakeet in a cage, a young woman at the window, a sailing ship outside in the harbour, or in the far distance, beyond fields and hedgerows, the foothills of the Vienna Woods – Nature domesticated. The view of Salzburg which Julius Schoppe painted in 1817 shows a small group of men gathered on a bench in the foreground – the artist and his comrades, like Lohbauer's Tübingen friends recognizable by their apparel as sympathizers of the progressive national cause. Yet what could possibly be improved upon in this perfectly ordered prospect? Framed by greenery, overarched by a radiant blue sky, it is the very image of perfection. A light veil of shadow lies across a field smooth as an English lawn below the terrace on which they are gathered to admire the view, and two tiny figures are walking along the path leading to Schloss Aigen, with the plains beyond gleaming in the sunlight; neatly clipped round trees line a long avenue, and beneath the castle the towers and houses of the city, surrounded by the wide blue arc of the mountains, shimmer in the sun. Exactly so, in Mörike's work *Das Stuttgarter Hutzelmännlein* [The Cobbler-Goblin of Stuttgart], the Schwäbische Alb appears, seen from the Bempflinger Höhe, as the wondrous glass-blue wall beyond which 'as he was told as a child, lie the cockle-shell gardens of the Queen of Sheba'. If we gaze into this safely bounded *orbis pictus* for long enough, we can easily imagine that here someone has stopped the clock and said: this is how it should be for ever after. The ideal world of the Biedermeier imagination is like a perfect world in miniature, a still life preserved under a glass dome. Everything in it seems to be holding its breath. If we turn it upside down, it begins to snow a little. Then all at once it becomes spring and summer again. It is impossible to imagine a more perfect order. And yet on either side of this apparently eternal calm there lurks the fear of the chaos of time spinning ever more rapidly out of control. When the young Mörike begins writing, he has at his back the revolutionary upheavals of the end of the eighteenth century, while the terrors which herald the new age of industrialization are already silhouetted on the horizon, the turmoil unleashed by the accumulation of capital and the moves towards centralization of a new, cast-iron state authority. The Swabian quietism Mörike subscribed to is – like all the Biedermeier arts – a kind of instinctive defence mechanism in the face of the calamity to come. In actual fact the everyday life of the time was far less secure than today's envious observer might imagine. Everywhere in the work of Grillparzer, Lenau and Stifter, dark abysses open up in their tales of family life: fear of bankruptcy, ruin, disgrace and *déclassement*. There are children who drown themselves in the Danube, brothers in prison or in the asylum, suicide and syphilis. Mörike, never far from the brink of financial ruin after he resigned his living as a vicar, knew from at least the age of thirteen – when his father died following a stroke – how precarious life in bourgeois society could be. His hypochondria, the mood-swings he was constantly prone to, his feelings of faint-heartedness, and the weariness of which he so often speaks; unspecified depressions, symptoms of paralysis, sudden weakness, vertigo, headaches, the terrors of uncertainty which he continually experiences – all these are symptoms not only of his melancholic disposition, but also the spiritual effects of a society increasingly determined by a work ethic and the spirit of competition. Things are sometimes so bad that he goes around 'like a frightened chicken' or 'a stupid child who cries at everything'. In his request to be released from his duties addressed to King Wilhelm I in 1843, he describes how at his last christening – after he had already had to call upon the assistance of a neighbouring cleric during the morning sermon – he suddenly felt so unwell that 'the congregation as well as I myself expected me to fall unconscious'. Mörike's fainting fits, and the impotence they express, are not least responses to the increasing consolidation of power in Germany, in the face of which he finds it ever more difficult to maintain his position in office, let alone hold his own as a poet in the new nation. Throughout his life he progressively retreats further and further from the exertions of artistic production, occupying himself with the revision of his novel, translating, busying himself with the composition of humorous poems and a long tail of occasional verses – engraved on a plant pot from Lorch for Wolff's wife; with the famous Schöntal recipe for pickled cucumbers for Constanze Hartlaub; on the occasion of the dedication of the Stuttgart Liederhalle,[6] and suchlike – and he doubtless often fears amid all this that he has lost sight of the true thread of his writing, and quite possibly he will soon be sitting up in bed, like his father after the stroke, with his pen in his trembling hand, searching for the right expression and completely incapable of finding it.

Plagued by inner anxieties and constrained economically – as he had been from the outset, and continued to be during his more than three decades as a retired minister – apart from two trips to Lake Constance and an excursion across the border into Bavaria, Mörike never, so far as I am aware, ventured beyond the narrow confines of his native Württemberg. Ludwigsburg, Urach, Tübingen, Pflummern, Plattenhardt, Ochsenwang, Cleversulzbach, Schwäbisch Hall, Nürtingen, Stuttgart and Fellbach[7] – these were his staging posts in an age otherwise in the grip of railway mania, stock market speculation, risky credit deals and general expansionism. The peaceful backwater of the Biedermeier age resembled a wishful utopia erected against progress, a painted screen disguising a world radically changing from the very foundations and opening up to new influences on all sides. Only once, as a young man, did Mörike venture beyond the limits of the kingdom of Württemberg, when he composed his South Sea fantasy – perfect for opera – of the land of Orplid. The inspiration for this draws less on the idea, by then almost forgotten, of the Noble Savage than it anticipates the era which Mörike almost lived to see, in which, in the new Imperial capital of Berlin, allotment settlements are created with names like *Frohe Eintracht* [Cheerful Harmony], *Ostelbien* [East of Elbe], *Alpenland* [Alpine Lands], and *Burenfarm* [Boer Farm], names which owe their origins not only to the expansion of the *Vaterland* from the Adige to the Belt,[8] but also to the colonialist aspirations to a German Africa and a German Tahiti. While Mörike was busy

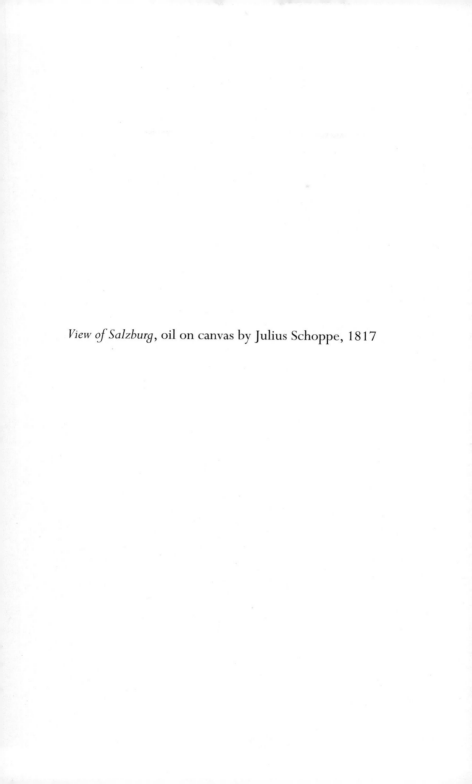

View of Salzburg, oil on canvas by Julius Schoppe, 1817

writing in Cleversulzbach or Schwäbisch Hall, the scale and proportions of the world were shifting in unpredictable ways. The Texan Consul had a villa built for himself among the Stuttgart vineyards,

and the Kingdom of Württemberg became an anachronism; it became necessary to think on a grand scale, and work *en miniature* was abandoned in favour of a monumentalism enacted ever more recklessly from decade to decade. Nor was Mörike's own writing unaffected by this development. His novel *Maler Nolten* [*Nolten the Painter*] is an experiment on a grand scale, in which over the course of several hundred pages an extraordinarily complex plot is unfolded. The young artist Theobald Nolten, as Birgit Mayer writes in her introductory book on Mörike, 'makes the acquaintance, via his former servant Wispel, of the newly successful artist Tillsen and sees his career advanced by the latter. Through Tillsen, Nolten is introduced to the society of Count Zerlin, and, believing himself deceived by the – alleged – infidelity of his fiancée, Agnes, falls in love with the Count's sister, Constanze. From this point on, fate takes its course. His relationship with Agnes had been on the one hand undermined by an intrigue on the part of the gypsy girl Elisabeth, yet on the other sustained – or so it appears – by a counter-intrigue in Nolten's name by his friend, the actor Larkens. The negative climax of the novel is reached when Constanze breaks with Nolten after finding out how things really stand. Verse interludes, a magic lantern show, and idyllic interpolations form a precarious counterbalance to the looming threat, but cannot avert it. In the further course of the action all the characters become ever more deeply enmeshed in secretive and tragic mutual dependencies, which in the end none of them survives.' From this deliberately abbreviated summary, which can scarcely begin to do justice to the emotional and social complexities involved, one may deduce that Mörike was beginning to lose his way in this ambitious undertaking, freighted as it was with subsidiary characters and episodes, interludes and subplots, and all manner of digressions and diversions. If his myopic eyes are often able to detect hidden wonders in the smallest detail, his eye grows dim if it falls on a wider panorama, and the twists and turns of fate which he invents for his characters soon dissolve into melodrama. 'The clock was just striking eleven. In the Zerlin household all had grown still, only in the bedroom of the Countess do we still find the lights burning. Constanze, in her white nightclothes, sitting alone at a small table near her bed, is busy letting down her beautiful hair, taking off her earrings and her delicate string of pearls, which always adorned her neck with such simple charm. Lost in thought, she held the necklace on her little finger up to the light, and if we rightly read her brow, it is Theobald of whom she is thinking . . . Restlessly she arose, restlessly she stepped to the window and let the magnificently bright heavens with all their portent, with all their splendour, act upon her. Her love for that man, from its first imperceptible stirrings to the astonishing state of her full aware-ness of it, from that moment in which her feelings had already become yearning and even desire to the pinnacle of the most power-ful passion – that whole range she now traversed in her mind and found it all beyond comprehension.' Immediately after this some-what dubious passage we learn of Nolten's 'irresistible ardour', of the 'full sweet ferment' of love which 'enveloped the senses' of the Countess in her remembered scene in the grotto; of 'the womb of an all-knowing fate', of 'ardent gratitude' and 'most heartfelt pleas'.[9] The inflamed passion of the elective affinities Mörike may have had in mind has inadvertently evolved into something precari-ously close to a better class of sensationalist romance, and among the vistas of parks and gardens which he has erected on the narra-tive stage, our Swabian vicar – who unfortunately is by no means at home in this aristocratic milieu – wanders around rather gloom-ily and just as aimlessly as poor Schubert in *Rosamunde* or in Berté's *Dreimäderlhaus*.[10] Like those of Mörike, Schubert's theatrical and operatic ambitions – which he hoped would lead to rapid success and at least a temporary relief from his financial dependence on his friends – often misfired, and, as on occasion in Mörike's poetry, so too in Schubert's works the most masterful strokes of genius are most readily to be found in the hidden shifts of his chamber music, for example the opening of the second movement of his last piano sonata, or in the song 'Die liebe Farbe' from *Die schöne Müllerin*; in those true *moments musicaux* where the iridescent chromatics begin to shimmer into dissonance, and an unexpected, even false change of key suddenly signals the abandoning of all hope, or, alternatively, grief gives way to consolation. Mainly it is the Moravian *Dorfmusikanten* [village musicians] whom one sees Schubert accompanying on their travels from village to village. He is more at home with them than he is toiling away at the high art which bourgeois notions of culture demand. Indeed, there is a portrait of Mörike

in which he looks almost exactly like the twin brother of the Viennese composer. Both were working at the same time, one looking out on to a Swabian apple orchard, the other in Himmelpfortgrund,[11] both attempting a form of composition which seeks to re-create, in a snatch of a half-vanished melody, that authentic *Volkston* which, in fact, has never existed as such.

So ist mein scheuer Blick,
Den schon die Ferne drängt,
Noch in das Schmerzensglück
Der Abschiedsnacht versenkt.

Dein blaues Auge steht
Ein dunkler See vor mir,
Dein Kuß, dein Hauch umweht
Dein Flüstern mich noch hier.

An deinem Hals begräbt
Sich weinend mein Gesicht,
Und Purpurschwärze webt
Mir vor den Augen dicht.

[Thus, while the distant view
Now claims my timid sight,
It dwells on leaving you:
That bitter joy, last night.

The dark lake of your eye
Still glimmers for me here,
Your kiss endures, your sigh,
Your whisper at my ear.

My weeping face still grieves
As on your breast it lies;
A purple blackness weaves
Its skein across my eyes.][12]

The mistake we always make as listeners is to imagine that these miracles of composition, language and music are drawing directly upon their natural heritage, whereas in fact they are the most artificial thing about it. What it takes to produce these effects remains, now as then, an undisclosed mystery. Certainly a rare adeptness at their craft, permitting the most minute adjustments and nuances; and then, or so I imagine, a very long memory and, possibly, a certain unluckiness in love, which appears to have been precisely the lot of those who, like Mörike and Schubert, Keller and Walser, have bequeathed to us some few of the most beautiful lines ever written.

Not for nothing is Mörike's work haunted by the spirit of the Swiss *vagabonde* Peregrina, whom at the time the young poet did not dare to stay with and whom he sent on her way 'in silence', as he remorsefully writes, 'into the wide grey world'.[13] For this enforced sacrifice of true love for the sake of the conventions of bourgeois society, which is the subject of the 'Peregrina' cycle and the echoes of which resonate now here, now there, in his work, Mörike pays for the rest of his life by the fact that he is surrounded by his mother, his sister, her friend his wife, and his daughters, trapped within an all-female household which is nothing more nor less than a travesty of the matriarchal order to which, at heart, all men long to return. This, it seems to me, is the subject of the *Historie der schönen Lau [Story of the Beautiful Lau]*, a water nymph with long flowing hair from the Danube delta exiled to the Blautopf near Ulm,[14] whose body resembles in all ways that of a natural woman, save that 'between her fingers and toes she has webbing white as blossom and more delicate than the petal of a poppy'. This fairytale, sprinkled with a number of obscure, almost surreal Swabian dialect words, such as *Schachzagel, Bartzefant, Lichtkarz, Habergeis* and *Alfanz*,[15] has as its matriarchal protagonist Frau Bertha Seysolffin, the stout landlady of the Nonnenhof, the inn at the former convent next to the Blautopf, who 'also is a true foster-mother to poor travelling journeymen'. In her garden 'the great golden pumpkins hang in autumn all the way down the slope to the pool.' Just next door is the monastery, where the men keep their own company. Sometimes it happens that the abbot comes out for a walk and takes a look to see if the landlady happens to be in her garden. On one such occasion in the story he also surprises her bathing in the Blautopf, greeting her with 'such a smacker of a kiss that it echoed off the church tower', reverberating all around, from the refectory, the stables, the fish house and the laundry, where it dingdongs back and forth between bucket and tub. Here, clearly, the right people have come together. At any rate one can easily imagine what act is being rung in by the great dingdong Mörike describes, even if, for the sake of decency, he glosses over the main action, noting only that the abbot, alarmed at the noise, rapidly waddled off. The fairytale happiness experienced by the two stout folk by the water's edge in Ulm harks back to a time when men and women were not bound to each other two by two, but merely appeared from time to time on the other's horizon, rather like the moon, which one doesn't see all the time either.

The story of the lovely Lau is, of course, a story within a story, built into another tale about Seppe, a shoemaker's journeyman apprentice from Stuttgart who one day leaves his home town and goes 'at first', as it says, 'as far as Ulm'. The story revolves around the fact that Seppe mixes up the two pairs of magic shoes given to him by the *Hutzelmännlein* – the eponymous 'cobbler-goblin' – one of which, the narrator reveals, 'is blessed and destined for a girl', with the result that on his journey he has great difficulty in walking. Only when he arrives back home in Stuttgart are the mismatched shoes reunited of their own accord with the feet that they are meant for, one happy pair on his own feet and the other on those of the girl Vrone, so that at the Stuttgart *Fastnacht* celebrations[16] these two Swabian protegés of the *Hutzelmännlein*, without any rehearsal, are able to perform acrobatic feats high above the heads of the crowd, so daring that 'it was as if they had been tightrope-walking all their lives'. All their actions, the narrator relates, 'seemed like a lovely web which they wove in time to the music'. 'Seppe,' so the story continues, 'as he danced did not look at the narrow rope beneath his feet, still less at the people below; he had eyes only for the girl – and when they both met in the centre he took her by the hands, they stood still and gazed fondly upon one another; and he was seen secretly to exchange a word with her. Then he suddenly leapt behind her and, turning their backs to each other, they stepped out in opposite directions. When he reached the crossing rod he stopped, waved his cap in the air and cried out heartily, "Long live all the ladies and gentlemen." Then the whole market cried out as one, *Vivat!*, three times, to each in turn. Amid all the noise and confusion and the fanfare of the trumpets, pipes and drums, Seppe ran across to Vrone, who was standing at the opposite end, caught her in his arms and kissed her for all the world to see.' In this fantasy of erotic wish-fulfilment in the dance of two beings high above the earthly sphere, risen above the abyss in which society cowers, a man who has long since given up on the idea of reciprocal love rather late in life imagines one last time how different things might have been if, at the time, he had run off with the by all accounts unusually beautiful and mysterious *vagabonde*, Maria Meyer, and pursued a different kind of mountebank career from that of writing – that rather vicarious vice whose clutches those who have once embarked upon it rarely succeed in escaping. And so we see Mörike at the last sitting in the garden surrounded by his wife's relations on a hot summer's day, the only one with a book in his hand, and in the end not very content in his role as a poet, from which he – unlike his clerical calling – can no longer retire. Still he has to torment himself with his novel and other such literary matters. But for years now the work has not really been going anywhere. The painter Friedrich Pecht, in a reminiscence from this time,

relates how on several occasions he observed Mörike noting down things which came into his head on special scraps and pieces of paper, only soon afterwards to take these notes and 'tear them up again into little pieces and bury them in the pockets of his dressing-gown'.

Death draws nigh
time marches on[1]

Some remarks on Gottfried Keller

I n no other literary work of the nineteenth century can the developments which have determined our lives even down to the present day be traced as clearly as in that of Gottfried Keller. When he started writing in the *Vormärz*,[2] hopes for a social contract were beginning to blossom, there was the governing of the people by the people still to be looked forward to, and everything could still have turned out differently from the way it actually did. True, republicanism was already starting to lose something of its former heroic character, and in many places those of a free-thinking disposition were beginning to succumb to the narrow-minded provincialism and petty parochial concerns which Nestroy pilloried so mercilessly in his dramas. Johannes Ruff's hand-coloured caricature of 1849, showing a well-organized *Freischar*, a troop of volunteers setting out on patrol, is, after all, scarcely a testament to political radicalism. Only two of the doughty men portrayed here have brought their weapons along; one, probably to help keep up his courage, is carrying a bottle of schnapps, while the mouse-like standard-bearer carries a ledger under his arm, and embroidered on his flag, as a fitting emblem for the entire movement, is a

brimming jug of ale. The short man beating the drum in the centre
is the poet himself, in the guise of an oddly civilian drum-major
wearing a top hat. Indeed, the whole scene has something distinctly
unmilitary and buttoned-up about it. It is difficult to imagine that
these five heroes are off to storm the barricades. Nor can it be a
coincidence that the motto inscribed in the upper-left-hand corner
of the picture reads 'By the right, quick marrrrch!' The comic
aspect of this scene, then, in a sense already anticipates the failure
of the revolution. When Keller was working on the first version
of *Der grüne Heinrich* [*Green Henry*] in Berlin in 1850, progress and
free-thinking had not been part of the Prussian agenda for quite
some time. The bourgeoisie had relinquished their political aspirations, and from then on concentrated exclusively on their business

interests, only engaging with the struggles for independence of other nations in their leisure time – if at all. Nevertheless, as Adolf Muschg has noted, from this north German perspective Switzerland could still be seen as 'the last bastion of European progress' and as 'the home of democracy, everywhere else misappropriated, betrayed and driven into exile'. Here in Switzerland, according to Muschg, 'March had been followed by a constitutional May, and economic and political liberalism (otherwise to be found only in the United States and in England) had successfully become established as guiding principles of the State.' When Keller returned to Zurich in the mid-1850s and was able to study this exemplary society at first hand, despite unreservedly identifying with the principle of the sovereignty of the people, he occasionally – and as time went on increasingly – began to have doubts about the direction events were taking, even in a state in which personal and political freedoms were guaranteed as of right. Among the outstanding German writers of the nineteenth century, Keller – along with the young Büchner – is perhaps the only one who had any grasp of political ideals and political pragmatism, and was therefore able to see that the gap between self-interest and the common good was growing ever wider, the emerging class of salaried workers was *de facto* excluded from the newly won rights and freedoms of the bourgeoisie, the term 'republic', as it says in *Martin Salander*,[3] had become nothing more than 'a stone given to the people in lieu of bread', and even the middle classes were being dealt a poor hand, inasmuch as the more political disillusionment increased, so too, in this phase of unregulated capitalism, did the constant anxiety as to the means of existence. Keller summarizes the history of the bourgeoisie synoptically, so to speak – from its fairytale and martial origins, via the age of Enlightenment, philanthropy and the self-confident *citoyen*, right down to the bourgeoisie concerned first and foremost with the preservation of their material possessions – in the well-known passage in which the tailor Wenzel Strapinski, wandering around the streets of Goldach, reads in amazement the names on the houses: The Pilgrim's Staff, The Bird of Paradise, The Water Nymph, The Pomegranate Tree, The Unicorn, The Iron Helmet, The Suit of Armour, The Crossbow, The Blue Shield, The Swiss Dagger: thus read the inscriptions on the oldest houses.[4] Then, in beautiful gold lettering, come the names *Eintracht* [Harmony], *Redlichkeit* [Honesty], *Liebe* [Charity], *Hoffnung* [Hope], *Recht* [Law] and *Landeswohl* [National Prosperity], while the more recent villas of the factory owners and bankers bear whimsical names straight out of an autograph album, such as *Rosental* [Rose Valley], *Veilchenberg* [Violet Hill][5] and *Jugendgarten* [Garden of Youth], or names which seem to hint at a substantial dowry, like *Henriettental* or *Wilhelminenburg*. Our tailor with his pin-pricked fingers feels very much a stranger in this small town which the narrator describes as a kind of moral Utopia, where the process of reification of our higher ideals and aspirations may literally be read from the walls and door frames of the buildings. The obverse of such prosperity, with its promise of happiness and enjoyment, so Wenzel Strapinski realizes as he stands at the crossroads looking back at the golden orbs on the towers gleaming enticingly through the trees, is freedom – so easily lost – but also work, privation, poverty and obscurity. Spectres such as these are everywhere in Keller's work. Acquainted with hardship from an early age through the death of his father, in retrospect his mother's meagre housekeeping, essentially consisting of almost nothing save frugality, becomes the epitome of an existence reduced to the barest minimum. 'The day after my departure, more than three years ago now,' writes the eponymous protagonist in *Der grüne Heinrich*, 'my mother had immediately altered her domestic arrangements and very nearly reduced them to the art of living on nothing. She invented a peculiar dish of her own, a species of black soup, which she made at midday, year in, year out, day after day the same, over a tiny fire, which likewise burnt practically nothing, and made one load of wood last an eternity. She did not set the table any more on weekdays, as she only ate alone now, to save not the trouble but the cost of washing the linen, and she placed her little dish upon a simple straw mat which always stayed clean, and while she dipped her worn three-quarters spoon into the soup, she regularly invoked the Almighty, asking him to give their daily bread to all, but particularly to her son.'[6] The art of making do with nothing which Keller describes here seems halfway to saintliness, and almost has the makings of a legend. Nevertheless, as the subtle ironic tone indicates, it does not so much present an alternative to the now all-pervasive principle of the accumulation of capital as serve precisely to exemplify it, albeit on the most modest of levels. Keller's critique of the economic system of *laissez-faire* was kindled by the fact that he was obliged to experience at first hand how what has been painstakingly saved up by means of self-denial is carried over to the next generation as debt, but it goes far beyond any personal sense of resentment, and is, rather, directed at the dangers – growing ever greater in proportion to the rapid increase in money in circulation – of a universal state of corruption. The *Ackerbürger* [city farmer] leaves his inherited property and comes to grief in the city, where – as one can read in *Martin Salander* – land and stock market speculation, mortgages and swindling are rife, like vine weevil and cholera, and every day clever folk are made fools of by the dozen and fools made into scoundrels. The semi-allegorical characters of Weidelich, Wohlwend and Schadenmüller stand for an entire class which now, hovering between rapidly acquired wealth and sudden ruin, threatens to sink wholesale into a hitherto unknown form of criminality. Towards the end of the novel, Martin Salander tells the story of a man sitting in a barber's shop who claims that, while he was having his beard trimmed, no fewer than four good acquaintances passed by on the street outside, 'each of whom at the present time had a relative in prison. That,' continued the barbered one, 'was rather too many during a single shave. And yet he had not, by far, seen all the people who passed by because the barber had pulled his face, by his nose-tip or chin, to one side every moment. He had perhaps overlooked several or had not recognized them because the blue screen on the window obscured the figures somewhat.' Looking at this episode, we can begin to form an idea of the dubious state of affairs prevailing in Zurich at the time. The benightedness of the citizens alluded to here, like the grating in front of the windows, is ominous enough. If anything more sinister, though, are the effects of such rampant capitalism on the natural environment. The very first page of *Martin Salander* informs us of 'the relentless building over of the earth', so that one now seeks in vain 'the traces of the old shady friendly paths which earlier had led upward between gently rolling meadows and gardens'. A little further on in the text we learn that, of the great trees which used to stand on the land adjoining the Salanders' house, only a single plane tree remains. 'What's become of the many fine trees which used to stand around the house?' Martin Salander, returning after a long absence, asks his wife. 'Did the owner have them cut down to be sold? The fool!' and she explains the matter to him as follows: 'Someone had taken the land away from him, or rather forced him to make building sites of it since several other landowners had had an unnecessary street laid. There it is, every green shade has disappeared and the ground changed into a sand and gravel surface. But no one comes to buy the lots.' Whereupon Salander comments: 'They are really scoundrels to wreck the climate for themselves like that.' It is almost as if one were reading a report from yesterday's newspaper. Not the least of Keller's achievements is that he was one of the first to recognize the havoc which the proliferation of capital inevitably unleashes upon the natural world, upon society, and upon the emotional life of mankind.

Friedrich Engels, in *The Origin of Private Property*, published in 1884,[7] put forward the view that the transition – long predating our historical memory, in an era shrouded in myth – from a matriarchal and polygamous society to a patriarchal and monogamous one was determined by the acquisition of property whose inheritance could only be assured with certainty by means of a system of monogamy. In accordance with this theory, in many ways still extremely plausible today, one might say that, even as high capitalism was spreading like wildfire in the second half of the nineteenth century, Keller in his work presents a counter-image of an earlier age, in which the relationships between human beings were not yet regulated by money. In one of his childhood reminiscences, Heinrich Lee recalls how, as a boy, he often used to spend time in a dark hall or warehouse filled with every kind of junk and bric-a-brac imaginable. And, as always when Keller has the opportunity of indulging his love for all things antique, there follows an incomparable description of all the outmoded, useless and arcane objects piled high on top of and in front of each other, beds and tables and all kinds of assorted implements, and how sometimes on the upper planes and slopes, and sometimes on the perilous lonely peaks of this bric-a-brac mountain,[8] here an ornate rococo clock and there a waxen angel lead a quiet and as it may be posthumous existence. In contrast to the continuous circulation of capital, these evanescent objects have been withdrawn from currency, having long since served their time as traded goods, and have, in some sense, entered eternity. The sovereign and soul of this empire of junk is a stout, elderly woman in an old-fashioned costume, who always sits in the same spot in her ill-lit emporium, and from there oversees a white-haired old man and a whole host of other underlings coming and going around the hall. She always wears snow-white sleeves pleated in the most artful way, after a fashion no longer seen any more. Not only in this does she somewhat resemble a priestess: the toings and froings before her armchair throne on the part of the male assistants and of the customers suggest that law and order are invested in her very person. As to a governor or to an abbess, we read, 'the people . . . would bring the most diverse gifts . . . field produce and tree fruit of every kind, milk, honey, grapes, ham and sausages are brought to her . . . and these stores are the foundation of a life of dignified ease.' Wonderful too is the passage where Keller describes how Frau Margret, who is scarcely able to decipher the printed word, and has never learned to reckon in Arabic numbers, using no more than four Roman numerals does her non-existent books with a piece of soft chalk on a large table-top by setting up long columns and, by means of a complicated series of transmutations, converts large sums of small amounts into smaller sums of larger denominations. Her system of signs and symbols, so the narrator tells us, would have appeared to any other observer like ancient heathen runes, and in truth Frau Margret, who is only interested in the Christian religion for its intercalated apocrypha and the speculations of the sectarians, seems to embody a much earlier stage of social development than that which had already been attained in her day. For this reason, the concept of capital is entirely alien to her. Any surplus she accumulates and does not need for immediate outgoings is taken out of the current purse, changed into gold, and put away in the treasure chest. It never occurs to her to let the capital work for her. It is true that she sometimes gives credit, but she does not lend money for interest. In the vaults of her emporium, then, we are a long way from the effects, so lamented by Keller, of the money market on the economic and moral constitution of his compatriots. The preference Keller shows here, in his portrait of Frau Margret, for a system of barter over trading for profit, reveals the extent of his aversion to the pace of developments taking place pell-mell all around him. It is, too, a particularly attractive trait in Keller's work that he should afford the Jews – whom Christianity has for centuries reproached with the invention of money-lending – pride of place in a story intended to evoke the memory of a pre-capitalist era. In the evening, when the warehouse is closed, Frau Margret's house becomes a kind of hostelry, offering shelter not just to favoured local people but to itinerant traders, for example the Jewish pedlars, like nomads still travelling with their wares from place to place, who, after setting down their heavy packs, without a word being spoken or a written pledge exchanged, entrust their purses to the landlady for safekeeping and stand at the stove brewing a coffee or baking a piece of fish. If then talk should turn among those present to the misdemeanours of the Hebrew peoples, to the abduction of children or the poisoning of wells, or if even Frau Margret herself should claim that she once saw the restless Ahasaver in person leaving the Black Bear where he had spent the night, the Jews merely listen to these scaremongering tales, smile good-humouredly and politely, and refuse to be provoked. This good-natured smile on the part of the Jewish traders at the credulity and foolishness of the unenlightened Christian folk, which Keller captures here, is the epitome of true tolerance: the tolerance of the oppressed, barely endured minority towards those who control the vagaries of their fate. The idea of tolerance, much vaunted in the wake of the Enlightenment but in practice always diluted, pales into insignificance beside the forbearance of the Jewish people. Nor do the Jews in Keller's works have any dealings with the evils of capitalism. What money they earn in their arduous passage from village to village is not immediately returned to circulation but is for the time being set to one side, thus becoming, like the treasure hoarded by Frau Margret, as insubstantial as gold in a fairytale. True gold, for Keller, is always that which is spun with great effort from next-to-nothing, or which glistens as a reflection above the shimmering landscape. False gold, meanwhile, is the rampant proliferation of capital constantly reinvested, the perverter of all good instincts. Keller warned early on against its temptations, and one can only speculate as to what he might have had to say about the shady deals perpetrated by the Swiss banks a mere two generations after his death, let alone about the gold, purchased at the expense of the immeasurable suffering of the Jews, which was to serve as a christening present for the generation of Swiss children born after the Second World War.

There is another way, too, in which the history of the Jews, as depicted in Keller's work, mirrors that of the people they live among. As a result of the political upheavals and the expansion of the market economy – which created at least as many bankrupts as it did *nouveaux riches* – all through the nineteenth century a growing number of Germans and Swiss found themselves forced to emigrate for a life in the diaspora, ending up just as far from home as any of the guests from the East in Frau Margret's house. For this reason, no doubt, in Ferdinand Kürnberger's novel of emigration the Germans are referred to as the Jews of America.[9] Only on foreign soil is it brought home to them what it means to be cut off from one's homeland and treated with contempt abroad. The fact that, after the failure of the 1848 revolution, 80,000 people emigrated to America from the region of Baden alone shows that the emigrants of that time were not merely adventurers, fortune seekers, or a few desperate individuals. Keller's analysis of this social phenomenon, too, is more accurate and more sympathetic than that of most of his literary contemporaries. While Heinrich Lee is learning about hardship first hand abroad, back at home meanwhile his uncle has died, his children long since scattered in the bustle and confusion of the highways, along which, he notes with characteristic irony, they went dragging their little ones in carts behind them as in former times the Children of Israel in the wilderness. Then there is the famous scene in which, standing to attention on the parade ground, Heinrich can only look on, his heart lurching in his breast, as the coach carrying the emigrants passes by, among them the woman who could have been mother, sister and lover to him. The chapter is entitled 'Judith goes too' ['Auch Judith geht']. The fact that this episode follows immediately upon Anna's funeral makes it clear that, for those left behind, Judith's departure too is like a death. Indeed, at that time it was generally as rare for emigrants to return home as for the dead to come back to life. For every one who, like Martin Salander, succeeded in making his fortune in Brazil, there were dozens who never managed to scrape together enough money working in the coffee plantations to pay their fare back home. Even Salander pays no small price for his success. Or we need only think of the young unmarried Swiss women, many of whom, as we know from the autobiographical writings of Conrad or Nabokov, could only find positions as governesses or tutors in lands far distant from their home cantons. Imagine their isolation as they stood gazing out of their windows at dusk, year after year, on some estate in the Ukraine or outside St Petersburg, for a moment believing that they could see, in the gathering clouds, a glimpse of the far-distant snow-white Alps. Fräulein Luise Rieter, for example, to whom Keller fruitlessly declared his affection, spent a long time in Paris and in the household of a doctor in Dublin. And how many more, down to and including Robert Walser and his siblings, did not end up scattered Lord knows where. In Keller's own case, his stays in Munich and Berlin were quite enough to give him a taste of the bitterness of exile. For this reason, Heinrich Lee's dreams of home, which take up a whole chapter and more in *Der grüne Heinrich*, are filled in equal measure with beauty and fear. He sees himself walking along the highway, staff in hand, and in the distance, on an interminable road which intersects with his own, catches sight of his long-dead father with a heavy knapsack on his back. Exile, as Keller describes it, is a form of purgatory located just outside this world. Anyone who has visited it will for ever after be a stranger in his own country. When, in his dream, Heinrich finally arrives back home and mounts the steps hand in hand with his childhood sweetheart, he finds all his relations assembled in the living room, his uncle, his aunt, all his cousins, the living and the dead together. Without exception they all wear contented, cheerful expressions, and yet this homecoming is anything but reassuring. Oddly, all those present are smoking long clay pipes filled with sweet-smelling tobacco, as a sign perhaps that in this in-between region different customs prevail. The way, too, in which they cannot stay still for a moment, but are compelled to wander ceaselessly up and down and back and forth while an assortment of animals — hunting dogs, martens, falcons and doves — scurry along the floor in the opposite direction: all of this strange and restless toing and froing would seem to suggest that these poor departed souls are anything but quiet and at one with their lot. Keller did, though, seek in another passage to rise above his fear that the return from exile, like exile itself, amounts to a premature encounter with death, in the wanderer fantasy where we see Heinrich Lee heading for home through a nocturnal Germany. 'I went through woods, across fields and meadows,' Lee writes, 'past villages whose dim outlines or faint lights lay far from my path. At midnight, as I was going over some wide open fields, the deepest solitude reigned over the earth, and the skies, interspersed with the slowly turning stars, became the more full of life, as invisible swarms of migratory birds passed high overhead with an audible rustling of wings.'

What is remarkable about this passage is the way in which Keller's prose, so unreservedly committed to earthly life, attains its most astonishing heights at precisely those moments where it reaches out to touch the edge of eternity. Anyone travelling along this path as it is unrolled before us, sentence after lovely sentence, over and over again senses with a shudder how deep is the abyss on either side, how sometimes the daylight seems to fade as the shadows gather from afar, and often is almost extinguished by the suggestion of death. There are many passages in Keller which could pass for the work of a baroque poet of mortality and *vanitas*. We need only think of Zwiehahn's wandering skull in Heinrich's luggage, the little ivory skeleton on the table of the Landvogt von Greifensee,[10] and the poet's mania for collecting, which sees him furnishing almost all his stories with a kind of treasure chest (or *Schatzkästlein*), in which, as in the cabinets of curiosities and jewel caskets of the seventeenth century, the most improbable relics co-exist side by side: a 'cherry stone carved with the passion of Christ, and a box made of filigree ivory inlaid with red taffeta, containing a little mirror and a silver thimble; further . . . another cherry stone wherein rattled a tiny game of ninepins, a walnut which when opened revealed a little image of the Virgin behind glass, a silver heart with a small perfumed

sponge inside, and a *bonbonnière* made of lemon peel with a straw-
berry painted on its lid, containing a golden pin on a piece of
cotton in the shape of a forget-me-not, and a medallion with a
monument of hair; further, a bundle of yellowed papers with
recipes and secrets, a bottle of Hoffmann's drops,[11] another of *eau
de Cologne* and a box with musk; another with a scrap of [pine]
marten dropping[12] in it, and a little basket plaited from fragrant
palm-leaves,[13] as well as one made of glass beads and cloves; finally
a little book with silver edges bound in sky-blue ribbed paper
and entitled *Golden Rules of Life for the Young Woman as Bride, Wife
and Mother*, and a small book of dreams, a guide to letter writing,
five or six love letters and a lancet for letting blood.' We find all
of this in the story of '*Die drei gerechten Kammacher*' ['*The Three
Righteous Combmakers*'],[14] in a lacquered chest belonging to Züs
Bünzlin which Wolfgang Schlüter, in his essay on Benjamin as
collector, refers to as a microcosmic *intérieur*. If the baroque
imagination, which we see here once more dwelling upon the
insignificant trifles we fashion and hoard during our brief time
on earth, itself already embodied a kind of vogue for death, then
its afterlife, as shown to us by Keller in this miniature world
within a world belonging to a Swiss spinster, is determined by a
narrative position which, as Wolfgang Schlüter writes, is circum-
spect even in its mockery, and whose underlying ironic
perspective – as Schlüter also notes – is derived not from distance,
but from painfully focused images viewed from the closest possible proximity. For this reason it would be wrong to see Keller as
a latterday preacher of death and damnation in disguise, even
though there can be no doubt that his inspiration derives from

the baroque tendencies still latent within him. What is unique about Keller's philosophy of transience is the serene glow with which it is suffused, stemming from the particular brand of *Weltfrömmigkeit* [secular piety] the young scholar from Zurich had become acquainted with during his time with the Heidelberg atheists. There were few things Keller could abide less than the self-righteous authority of religion, nothing he loathed more than the bigotry that seeks to wield the rod to make of poor little Meret an honest Christian child.[15] This liberation from the age-old prison of religion is what lets in the light which he sees illumining even the darkest hours. There can scarcely be a brighter eulogy than the funeral oration which Heinrich holds for his young cousin Anna, who passed away long before her time. When the carpenter is rubbing down her newly finished coffin with pumice, Heinrich recalls, it becomes 'as white as snow, and only the very faintest reddish touch of the fir shone through, giving the tint of apple blossom. It looked far more beautiful and dignified than if it had been painted, gilded, or even brass-bound. At the head, the carpenter had according to custom constructed an opening with a sliding cover through which the face could be seen until the coffin was lowered into the grave; now there still had to be set in a pane of glass which had been forgotten, and I rowed home to get one. I knew that on top of a cupboard there lay a small old picture-frame from which the picture had long since disappeared. I took the glass that had been forgotten, placed it carefully in the boat, and rowed back. The carpenter was roaming about a little in the woods looking for hazelnuts; meanwhile, I tested the pane of glass, and when I found that it fitted the opening, I dipped it in the clear stream, for it was covered with dust, and clouded, and with care I succeeded in washing it without breaking it on the stones. Then I lifted it and let the clear water run off it, and when I held up the shining glass high against the sun and looked through it, I saw three boy-angels making music; the middle one was holding a sheet of music and singing, the other two were playing old-fashioned violins, and they were all looking upwards in joy and devotion; but the vision was so thinly and delicately transparent that I did not know whether it was hovering in the rays of the sun, in the glass, or merely in my imagination. When I moved the glass, the angels instantly vanished, until suddenly, turning the glass another way, I saw them again. Since then I have been told that copper-plate engravings or drawings which have lain undisturbed for a great many years behind a glass communicate themselves to the glass during these years, in the dark nights, and leave behind upon it something like a reflected image.' The solace Heinrich derives from this chapter of his life story has nothing to do with hope for eternal bliss, as might perhaps initially appear to be the case. The angels with their gaze turned heavenwards are only an illusion, virtual vignettes giving the appearance of a miracle which is, in fact, merely the result of a chemical reaction. Rather, Keller achieves this reconciliation with death in a purely earthly realm: in the satisfaction of work well done, in the snowy gleam of the fir wood, the peaceful boat journey across the lake with the pane of glass, and in the perception, through the gradually lifting veil of mourning, of the beautiful clarity, undimmed by any hint of transcendence, of the air, the light and the pure shining water.

This attachment to earthly life is borne out by the fact that nowhere in these stories of Keller's does the desire for redemption emerge more clearly than in the repeatedly imagined evocation — quite contrary to Keller's own experience — of the consummation of love. Just as Heinrich, on his nocturnal walk with Judith, listens eagerly to the rustle of her dress and every few moments feels the need to glance furtively across at her 'like a fearful pilgrim at whose side walks a spectre of the woods', so too Keller's gaze, as he writes, is always directed at the unknown and mysterious nature of woman, who only becomes truly familiar to him as a figment of the imagination. The scenes where the lovers are united, which he pictures in such loving detail, are not only among the most touching in literature; they are unique, too, inasmuch as in them desire is not immediately betrayed by the fixed masculine gaze. It says much that in Keller's work the true lover is barely more than a child, for example the young Heinrich Lee in the chapter where, locked in the theatre overnight, still wearing his monkey costume and with Mephistopheles' cloak around his shoulders, he wanders around by moonlight on the stage amid all the rustling paper splendours, raising the curtain, and in the orchestra pit, at first tentatively and then with increasing force, begins to make the kettledrums roll until finally a veritable crescendo of thunder echoes through the darkened auditorium, and rouses the beautiful actress who shortly before has breathed her last upon the boards. 'It was Gretchen, just as I had last seen her,' thus Lee in his recollection of his theatrical adventures as a monkey. 'I shuddered from head to foot, my teeth chattered, and yet at the same time a powerful sensation of joyful surprise flashed through me and made me glow. Yes, it was Gretchen, it was her spirit, although the distance was too great for me to distinguish her features, making the apparition seem even more ghostly. With mysterious gaze, she appeared to be searching the hall; I pulled myself upright, I was drawn forward as if by powerful, invisible hands, and, my heart beating audibly, I stepped over the benches towards the front of the stage, pausing at every step. The fur covering muffled my footsteps so that the figure did not notice me until, as I climbed up to the prompter's box, the first moonbeam fell like a streak across my strange costume. I saw how she fixed her glowing eyes on me, horrified, and then shrank back in alarm, but silently. I trod one quiet step nearer, and halted again; my eyes were opened wide, I held my trembling hands aloft while, a glad fire of courage running through my veins, I made for the phantom. Then it called out imperiously: "Halt! You little creature, what are you?" stretching out its arms threateningly against me so that I stood still, rooted to the spot. We looked fixedly at each other; I recognized her features now. She was wrapped in a white nightdress, her neck and shoulders were bare and gleamed softly, like snow by night.' Adolf Muschg has said of Keller that it would have required a miracle of empathy and consideration to overcome the feelings of social and physical inferiority from which he suffered. This scene in the theatre presents us with just such a miracle. The actress removes the little creature's mask, enfolds him closely in her arms and kisses him repeatedly on the lips, because, as she says afterwards, he has not yet become the rogue he will turn into later, just like all the others, once he has grown up. The tender consummation of this childlike desire for love is soon followed

Ideal Landscape with Trees, Gottfried Keller, 1849

by a scarcely less easeful death. Gretchen takes the monkey into her bed, where the two fall peacefully asleep,[16] she shrouded in a royal velvet cloak and Heinrich sewn into his fur costume, thus bearing, as the narrator says, no small resemblance to those monumental tombs 'where a knight of stone lies at full length, his faithful dog at his feet'. The vision here is of the body turned to stone at the moment of utmost happiness, a petrifaction which is a symbol not of punishment or banishment, but an expression of the hope that the moment of supreme bliss might last for ever. Another, scarcely less peaceful end seems assured for the tailor Strapinski, far from home in Switzerland, when, his secret having been revealed by the charade acted out by his *Doppelgänger*, filled with a sense of shame he walks out into the winter night where presently, overcome by 'the fiery drinks consumed and his grievous stupidity', he sinks down by the side of the road and falls asleep 'on the crisp frozen snow, while an icy wind begins to blow from the east'. Wenzel Strapinski's rescue from an already certain death, as Keller then describes it, runs counter to all the prevailing erotic conventions of bourgeois literary tradition. Whereas, in the *Novelle* from Kleist to Schnitzler, it is invariably the male hero who, in an attitude of macabre lust, is to be found bending over the unconscious or lifeless body of a woman, in Keller's tale it is the female gaze of Nettchen which is permitted to rove uninhibitedly over the graceful and noble body of the tailor with his slender, supple limbs and (as it tellingly says) tightly laced form. And when, by means of energetic rubbing, Nettchen finally succeeds in massaging the limp and almost lifeless tailor back to life and he slowly sits up, it becomes abundantly clear that Keller's erotic longings were directed towards a reversal of the prevailing gender roles as prescribed by society. Possibly for this reason we are informed, in the following passage, that Wenzel Strapinski had, during his time in the military, served with the Hussars, and worn one of those splendidly colourful uniforms as sported by that ideal masculine type for which women have pined right up to the twentieth century. The source of Keller's identification with feminine desire cannot, though, be determined with any certainty. Walter Benjamin believed that 'Keller's gloomy composure is based on the profound equilibrium that the masculine and feminine sides of his being have reached,' arguing that this also relates to the poet's facial appearance. In this context Benjamin goes on to comment on the history of the androgynous type in Greek antiquity, referring to the figure of Aphroditos – the bearded Aphrodite – and the Argive women whose custom it was to adorn themselves with a false beard on their wedding night. If we look closely at the drawings which Johann Salomon Hegi made of

Keller at twenty-one, his eyelids lowered in sleep, with his long eyelashes and uncommonly sensual lips, it is not difficult to agree with Benjamin when he states that the idea of such androgynous faces 'brings us closer than anything else to the face of this poet'.[17]

Keller's love stories, though, do not always end so happily (or so hopelessly) as that of the Polish tailor who, after his fortunate rescue, still has a long and by no means enchanted career ahead of him. Indeed, the two 'village children' Sali and Vrenchen, lacking the slightest means of support, really do forfeit their lives. The barge laden with hay on which, after their journey on foot through the homeland in which they are now strangers, they finally consummate their love, towards the end of the story swings out into the current and floats, slowly turning, downriver towards the valley. 'Sometimes the river glided through tall dark forests that laid their shade upon it; sometimes it flowed past open fields; now silent villages slid by it, and now a lonely hut; here it widened into an expanse like the bosom of a lake, and the boat almost ceased to move; there the current rushed around great rocks and sped on swiftly by the sleeping shores. In the first flush of dawn a town with many towers rose up out of the silvery waters, while low down in the sky a red-gold moon laid its path upon the river. Down this path the boat drifted slowly sideways, and as it neared the wharfs of the town, in the frosty autumn mist two figures, closely clasped, slipped over the side of the dark hulk and were swept beneath the bitter current.'[18] Glide, flow, rush, pause, rise up, clasp, slip – these are the verbs by means of which, in this passage, a metaphor is gradually crafted for the physical act of love being consummated with every twist and turn of the boat and of the sentences, a love which Keller, who on paper at least can determine their fate, bequeaths the youngsters from the village as their rightful due, even though – so far as anyone can tell – he never experienced such fulfilment himself. From the very beginning, despite a deep need of and evidently inexhaustible capacity for love, Keller's life was marked by rejection and disappointment. The ladies whose hand he sought were not easily able to overlook his short stature, not Fräulein Rieter, nor the beautiful woman from the Rhineland whom he so admired as she rode along the Berlin boulevards, nor the Heidelberg actress Johanna Kapp. And Luise Scheidegger, the only one who was prepared to share her life with Keller, a few weeks after their engagement drowned herself in a fountain in Herzogenbuchsee. In his darker moments, Keller may well have seen this as proof that he was not wrong to be ashamed of his ill-proportioned body, so to speak not fully developed from the waist down, and that he was destined to bring despair upon those to whom he declared his love. The actress from Heidelberg, too, ended her days in mental darkness. In the Zurich Central Library there is a small watercolour by Keller of an idealized landscape with trees, which – via the painter Bernhard Fries, a member of the Feuerbach circle – came into the possession of Johanna Kapp, who during her illness cut away, in a minute and detailed operation, approximately a quarter of the lower part of the picture. What moved her to this drastic incision, we do not know, nor what Keller's feelings were when, after its return to him following Johanna's death, he held the thus disfigured picture in his hands once more. But perhaps he may have sensed that the snow-white space which opens up behind the almost transparent landscape is even more beautiful than the coloured miracle of art. At any rate, the antithesis to this glimpse into a beyond consisting of pure nothingness, revealed by the unfortunate Johanna's scissorwork, is the colossal scrawl[19] which Heinrich Lee one day, in a melancholy moment, begins to execute on a large piece of cardboard, and which he continues each day with countless strokes of the pen until a vast grey cobweb covers almost the entire surface. 'If you observed,' writes Heinrich, 'the tangle more closely, you could discover therein the most commendable coherence and application, as it formed a labyrinth which could be followed up from the starting point to the end, in a continuous progression of strokes and windings which perhaps amounted to thousands of yards. At times a new style manifested itself, to a certain degree a new epoch of the work; new designs and motifs, often delicate and graceful, appeared, and if the amount of attention, sense of the appropriate, and perseverance that was required for this absurd mosaic had been applied to a real task, I certainly should have produced something worth looking at. Here and there only, hesitations, smaller or greater, appeared, certain twists in the labyrinths of my distracted soul, and the careful manner in which the pen had sought to extricate itself from the dilemma proved how my dreaming consciousness was caught in the web. So it went on for days and weeks, and the sole variation, when I was at home, would be that, with my forehead leaning against the window, I would watch the progress of the clouds, observe their shape, and in the meantime let my thoughts rove afar into the distance.' This description of the distinctly melancholic scrawl is reminiscent of the blue sheets of paper which Keller used as blotters as he toiled over his *Bildungsroman* at his desk in Berlin, and which over and over again repeat the name of his unrequited love in long intricately

entwined lines, swirls, columns and loops in a myriad variations –
Betty Betty Betty, BBettytybetti, bettibettibetti, Bettybittebetti
[Bettypleasebetti] is scrawled and doodled there in every calli-
graphic permutation imaginable. And around and between these
five or six letters there is nothing, save here and there a sketch
of a gateway to a walled garden, also with Betty inscribed above
it, a Betty-mirror, a Betty-room and a Betty-clock and next to it
a Reaper, and another skeleton playing the fiddle, a funeral bell,
and a kind of miniature coat of arms in which, through a magnifying glass, something can be made out which looks like a heart
pierced through with pins. The art of writing is the attempt to
contain the teeming black scrawl which everywhere threatens to
gain the upper hand, in the interests of maintaining a halfway

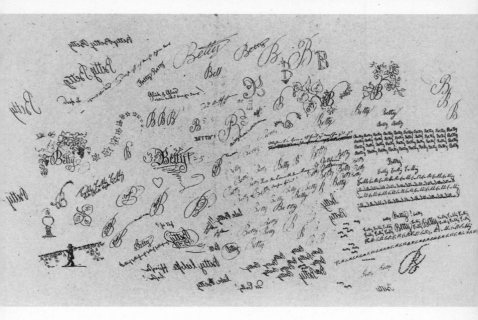

functional personality. For many years Keller subjected himself to this difficult task, even though he was aware early on that it was to no avail. The 'somewhat melancholy and monosyllabic official', who says at the end of his novel that nothing can now lighten the shadows which fill his desolate soul, already suspects that even the best arrangement of letters and sentences on the page, like the generosity he showed towards his characters, in the long term counts for little when set against the heavy burden of disappointment. Looking back on his career, he feels that all of this 'was no life, and could not go on thus'. He speaks of a new imprisonment of the spirit in which he has become entrapped, and broods as to the means of escaping it, but so hopeless does his situation appear that from time to time, and ever more distinctly, as he says, there stirs in him the wish no longer to exist at all.

Le promeneur solitaire

A remembrance of Robert Walser

The traces Robert Walser left on his path through life were so faint as to have almost been effaced altogether. Later, after his return to Switzerland in the spring of 1913, but in truth from the very beginning, he was only ever connected with the world in the most fleeting of ways. Nowhere was he able to settle, never did he acquire the least thing by way of possessions. He had neither a house, nor any fixed abode, nor a single piece of furniture, and as far as clothes are concerned, at most one good suit and one less so. Even among the tools a writer needs to carry out his craft were almost none he could call his own. He did not, I believe, even own the books that he had written. What he read was for the most part borrowed. Even the paper he used for writing was secondhand. And just as throughout his life he was almost entirely devoid of material possessions, so too he was remote from other people. He became more and more distant from even the siblings originally closest to him – the painter Karl and the beautiful schoolteacher Lisa – until in the end, as Martin Walser said of him, he was the most unattached of all solitary poets. For him, evidently, coming to an arrangement with a woman was an impossibility. The chambermaids in the Hotel zum Blauen Kreuz, whom he used to watch through a peephole he had had bored in the wall of his attic lodgings; the serving girls in Berne; Fräulein Resy Breitbach in the Rhineland, with whom he maintained a lengthy correspondence – all of them were, like the ladies he reveres so longingly in his literary fantasias, beings from a distant star. At a time when large families were still the norm – Walser's father, Adolf, came from a family of fifteen – strangely enough none of the eight siblings in the next generation of Walsers brought a child into the world; and of all this last generation of Walsers, dying out together, as it were, none was perhaps less suited to fulfil the prerequisites for successful procreation than Robert, who, as one may say in his case with some fittingness, retained his virginal innocence all his life. His death – the death of one who, inevitably rendered even more anonymous after the long years in an institution, was in the end connected to almost nothing and nobody – might easily have passed as unnoticed as, for a long time, had his life. That Walser is not today among the forgotten writers we owe primarily to the fact that Carl Seelig took up his cause. Without Seelig's accounts of the walks he took with Walser, without his preliminary work on the biography, without the selections from the work he published and the lengths he went to in securing the *Nachlaß* – the writer's millions of illegible ciphers – Walser's rehabilitation could never have taken place, and his memory would in all probability have faded into oblivion. None the less, the fame which has accrued around Walser since his posthumous redemption cannot be compared with that of, say, Benjamin or Kafka. Now, as then, Walser remains a singular, enigmatic figure. He refused by and large to reveal himself to his readers. According to Elias Canetti, what set Walser apart from other writers was the way in which, in his writing, he always denied his innermost anxieties, constantly omitting a part of himself. This absence, so Canetti claimed, was the source of his unique strangeness. It is odd, too, how sparsely furnished with detail is what we know of the story of his life. We know that his childhood was overshadowed by his mother's melancholia and by the decline of his father's business year after year; that he wanted to train as an actor; that he did not last long in any of his positions as a clerk; and that he spent the years from 1905 to 1913 in Berlin. But what he may have been doing there apart from writing – which at the time came easily to him – about that we have no idea at all. So little does he tell us about the German metropolis, so little, later, of the Seeland around Biel and his years there, and his circumstances in Berne, that one might almost speak of a chronic impoverishment of experience. External events, such as the outbreak of the First World War, appear to affect him hardly at all. The only certain thing is that he writes incessantly, with an ever increasing degree of effort; even when the demand for his pieces slows down, he writes on, day after day, right up to the pain threshold and often, so I imagine, a fair way beyond it. When he can no longer go on we see him in the Waldau clinic, doing a bit of work in the garden or playing a game of billiards against himself, and finally we see him in the asylum in Herisau, scrubbing vegetables in the kitchen, sorting scraps of tinfoil, reading a novel by Friedrich Gerstäcker or Jules Verne, and sometimes, as Robert Mächler relates, just standing stiffly in a corner. So far apart are the scenes of Walser's life which have come down to us that one cannot really speak of a story or of a biography at all, but rather, or so it seems to me, of a legend. The precariousness of Walser's existence – persisting even after his death – the emptiness blowing through every part of it, lends it an air of spectral insubstantiality which may deter the professional critics just as much as the indefinability of the texts. No doubt Martin Walser[1] is correct in remarking that Robert Walser – despite the fact that his work seems positively to invite dissertation – always eludes any kind of systematic treatment. How is one to understand an author who was so beset by shadows and who, none the less, illumined every page with the most genial light, an author who created humorous sketches from pure despair, who almost always wrote the same thing and yet never repeated himself, to whom his own thoughts, honed on the tiniest details, became incomprehensible, who had his feet firmly on the ground yet was always getting lost in the clouds, whose prose has the tendency to dissolve upon reading, so that only a few hours later one can barely remember the ephemeral figures, events and things of which it spoke. Was it a lady named Wanda or a wandering apprentice, Fräulein Elsa or Fräulein Edith, a steward, a servant or Dostoyevsky's *Idiot*, a conflagration in the theatre or an ovation, the Battle of Sempach, a slap in the face or the return of the Prodigal, a stone urn, a suitcase, a pocket watch or a pebble?[2] Everything written in these incomparable books has – as their author might himself have said – a tendency to vanish into thin air. The very passage which a moment before seemed so significant can suddenly appear quite unremarkable. Conversely, Walser's *sottises* often conceal the profoundest depths of meaning. Despite such difficulties, however, which seem designed to foil the plans of anyone intent on categorization, much has been written about Robert Walser. Most of it, admittedly, is of a rather impressionistic or marginal nature, or can be regarded as an act of *hommage* on the part of his admirers. Nor are the remarks which follow any exception, for since my first encounter with Walser I too have only ever

been able to read him in an unsystematic fashion. Beginning now here and now there, for years I have been roaming around, now in the novels, now in the realms of the *Bleistiftgebiet* [Pencil Regions],[3] and whenever I resume my intermittent reading of Walser's writings, so too I always look again at the photographs we have of him, seven very different faces, stations in a life which hint at the silent catastrophe that has taken place between each.

The pictures I am most familiar with are those from his time in Herisau, showing Walser on one of his long walks, for there is something in the way that the poet, long since retired from the service of the pen, stands there in the landscape that reminds me instinctively of my grandfather, Josef Egelhofer, with whom

as a child I often used to go for walks for hours at a time during those very same years, in a region which is in many ways similar to that of Appenzell. When I look at these pictures of him on his walks, the cloth of Walser's three-piece suit, the soft collar, the tie-pin, the liver-spots on the back of his hands, his neat salt-and-pepper moustache and the quiet expression in his eyes — each time I think I see my grandfather before me. Yet it was not only in their appearance that my grandfather and Walser resembled each other, but also in their general bearing, something about the way each had of holding his hat in his hand, and the way that, even in the finest weather, they would always carry an umbrella or a raincoat. For a long time I even imagined that my grandfather shared with Walser the habit of leaving the top

button of his waistcoat undone. Whether or not that was actually the case, it is a fact that both died in the same year, 1956 — Walser, as is well known, on a walk he took on the 25th of December, and my grandfather on the 14th of April, the night before Walser's last birthday, when it snowed once more even though spring was already underway. Perhaps that is the reason why now, when I think back to my grandfather's death – to which I have never been able to reconcile myself – in my mind's eye I always see him lying on the horn sledge on which Walser's body, after he had been found in the snow and photographed, was taken back to the asylum. What is the significance of these similarities, overlaps and coincidences? Are they rebuses of memory, delusions of the self and of the senses, or rather the schemes and symptoms of an order underlying the chaos of human relationships, and applying equally to the living and the dead, which lies beyond our comprehension? Carl Seelig relates that once, on a walk with Robert Walser, he had mentioned Paul Klee – they were just on the outskirts of the hamlet of Balgach – and scarcely had he uttered the name than he caught sight, as they entered the village, of a sign in an empty shop window bearing the words *Paul Klee – Carver of Wooden Candlesticks*. Seelig does not attempt to offer an explanation for the strange coincidence. He merely registers it, perhaps because it is precisely the most extraordinary things which are the most easily forgotten. And so I too will just set down without comment what happened to me recently while reading the novel *Der Räuber* [*The Robber*], the only one of Walser's longer works with which I was at the time still unfamiliar.[4] Quite near the beginning of the book the narrator states that the Robber crossed Lake Constance by moonlight. Exactly thus – by moonlight – is how, in one of my own stories, Aunt Fini imagines the young Ambros crossing the selfsame lake, although, as she makes a point of saying, this can scarcely have been the case in reality. Barely two pages further on, the same story relates how, later, Ambros, while working as a room service waiter at the Savoy in London, made the acquaintance of a lady from Shanghai, about whom, however, Aunt Fini knows only that she had a taste for brown kid gloves and that, as Ambros once noted, she marked the beginning of his *Trauerlaufbahn* [career in mourning]. It is a similarly mysterious woman clad all in brown, and referred to by the narrator as the Henri Rousseau woman, whom the Robber meets, two pages on from the moonlit scene on Lake Constance, in a pale November wood – and nor is that all: a little later in the text, I know not from what depths, there appears the word *Trauer-laufbahn*, a term which I believed, when I wrote it down at the end of the Savoy episode, to be an invention entirely my own. I have always tried, in my own works, to mark my respect for those writers with whom I felt an affinity, to raise my hat to them, so to speak, by borrowing an attractive image or a few expressions, but it is one thing to set a marker in memory of a departed colleague, and quite another when one has the persistent feeling of being beckoned to from the other side.

Who and what Robert Walser really was is a question to which, despite my strangely close relationship with him, I am unable to give any reliable answer. The seven photographic portraits of him, as I have said, show very different people; a youth filled with a quiet sensuality; a young man hiding his anxieties as he prepares to make his way in bourgeois society; the heroic-looking writer of brooding aspect in Berlin; a 37-year-old with pale, watery-clear eyes; the Robber, smoking and dangerous-looking; a broken man; and finally the asylum inmate, completely destroyed and at the same time saved. What is striking about these portraits is not only how much they differ from each other, but also the palpable incongruity inherent in each — a feature which, I conjecture, stems at least in part from the contradiction between Walser's native Swiss reserve and utter lack of conceit, and the anarchic, bohemian and dandyesque tendencies he displayed at the beginning of his career, and which he later hid, as far as possible, behind a façade of solid respectability. He himself relates how one Sunday he walked from Thun to Berne wearing a 'louche pale-yellow summer suit and dancing pumps' and on his head a 'deliberately dissolute, daring, ridiculous hat'. Sporting a cane, in Munich he promenades through the Englischer Garten to visit Wedekind, who shows a lively interest in his loud check suit — quite a compliment, considering the extravagant fashions in vogue among the Schwabinger *bohème* at the time. He describes the walking outfit he wore on the long trek to Würzburg as having a 'certain southern Italian appearance. It was a sort or species of suit in which I could have been seen to advantage in Naples. In reasonable, moderate Germany, however, it seemed to arouse more suspicion than confidence, more repulsion than attraction. How daring and fantastical I was at twenty-three!' A fondness for conspicuous costume and the dangers of indigence often go hand in hand. Hölderlin, too, is said to have had a definite penchant for fine clothes and appearance, so that his dilapidated aspect at the beginning of his breakdown was all the more alarming to his friends. Mächler recalls how Walser once visited his brother on the island of Rügen wearing threadbare and darned trousers, even though the latter had just made him a present of a brand-new suit, and in this context cites a passage of *Die Geschwister Tanner* [*The Tanners*] in which Simon is reproached by his sister thus: 'For example, Simon, look at your trousers: All ragged at the bottom! To be sure, and I know this perfectly well myself: they're just trousers, but trousers should be kept in just as good a condition as one's soul, for when a person wears torn, ragged trousers it displays carelessness, and carelessness is an attribute of the soul. Your soul must be ragged too.' This reproach may well go back to remarks Lisa was at times wont to make about her brother's appearance, but the inspired turn of phrase at the end – the reference to the ragged soul – that, I think, is an original aperçu on the part of the narrator, who is under no illusion as to how things stand with his inner life. Walser must at the time have hoped, through writing, to be able to escape the shadows which lay over his life from the beginning, and whose lengthening he anticipates at an early age, transforming them on the page from something very dense to something almost weightless. His ideal was to overcome the force of gravity. This is why he had no time for the grandiose tones in which the 'dilettantes of the extreme left', as he calls them, were in those days proclaiming the revolution in art. He is no Expressionist visionary prophesying the end of the world, but rather, as he says in the introduction to *Fritz Kochers Aufsätze* [Fritz Kocher's Essays], a clairvoyant of the small.[5] From his earliest attempts on, his natural inclination is for the most radical minimization and brevity, in other words the possibility of setting down a story in one fell swoop, without any deviation or hesitation. Walser shares this ambition with the Jugendstil artists, and like them he is also prone to the opposite tendency of losing himself in arabesques. The playful – and sometimes obsessive – working in with a fine brush of the most abstruse details is one of the most striking characteristics of Walser's idiom. The word-eddies and turbulence created in the middle of a sentence by exaggerated participial constructions, or conglomerations of verbs such as 'haben helfen dürfen zu verhindern' ['have been able to help to prevent']; neologisms, such as for example 'das Manschettelige' [cuffishness] or 'das Angstmeierliche' [chicken-heartedness], which scuttle away under our gaze like millipedes; the 'night-bird shyness, a flying-over-the-seas-in-the-dark, a soft inner whimpering'[6] which, in a bold flight of metaphor, the narra-tor of *The Robber* claims hovers above one of Dürer's female figures; deliberate curiosities such as the sofa 'squeaching' ['gyxelnd'] under the charming weight of a seductive lady; the regionalisms, redolent of things long fallen into disuse; the almost manic loquaciousness – these are all elements in the painstaking process of elaboration Walser indulges in, out of a fear of reach-ing the end too quickly if – as is his inclination – he were to set down nothing but a beautifully curved line with no distracting branches or blossoms. Indeed, the detour is, for Walser, a matter of survival. 'These detours I'm making serve the end of filling time, for I really must pull off a book of considerable length, otherwise I'll be even more deeply despised than I am now.' On the other hand, however, it is precisely these linguistic montages – emerging as they do from the detours and digressions of narra-tive and, especially, of form – which are most at odds with the demands of high culture. Their associations with nonsense poetry and the word-salad symptomatic of schizophasia were never likely to increase the market value of their author. And yet it is precisely his uniquely overwrought art of formulation which true readers would not be without for the world, for example in this passage from the *Bleistiftgebiet* which, comic and heartbreaking in equal measure, condenses a whole romantic melodrama into the space of a few lines. What Walser achieves here is the complete and utter subjection of the writer to the language, a pretence at awkwardness brought off with the utmost virtuosity, the perfect realization of that irony only ever hinted at by the German Romantics yet never achieved by any of them – with the possible exception of Hoffmann – in their writings. 'In vain,' the passage in question tells us, regarding the beautiful Herta and her faithless Italian husband, 'did she buy, in the finest first-class boutiques, for her most highly respected darling rake and pleasure-seeker, a new walking cane, say, or the finest and warmest coat which she could find, procure or purchase. His heart remained indifferent beneath the carefully chosen item of clothing and the hand hard which held the cane, and while this scoundrel – oh that we might be permitted to call him thus – frivolously flitted or flirted around, there trickled from those big tragic eyes, embellished by heartache with dark rims, heavy tears like pearls, and here we must remark, too, that the rooms where such intimate misfortune was played out were fairly brimming with gloomy, fantastically be-palmleaved decoration gilded further by the height and scale of the whole.' 'Little sentence, little sentence' – so Walser concludes this escapade which is all but grammatically derailed by the end, 'you seem to me phantastical as well, you do!' And then, coming down to earth, he adds the sober phrase, 'But let us continue.'

But let us continue. As the fantastical elements in Walser's prose works increase, so too their realistic content dwindles – or, rather, reality rushes past unstoppably as in a dream, or in the cinema. Ali Baba, quite hollowed out by unrequited love and pious devotion to duty in the diligent service of the most cruel of all princesses, and in whom we may easily recognize one of Walser's alter egos – Ali Baba one evening sees a long sequence of cinematic images unfold before his eyes: naturalistic landscapes like the many-peaked Engadin, the Lac de Bienne and the Kurhaus at Magglingen. 'One after another,' the story continues, 'there came into view a Madonna holding a child on her arm, a snowfield high in the Alps, Sunday pleasures by the lakeside, baskets of fruit and flower arrangements, all of a sudden a painting representing the kiss Judas gave Jesus in the Garden of Gethsemane, with his fat face, round as an apple, almost preventing him from carrying out his plan; then a scene from a *Schützenfest*,[7] and, civility itself, a collection of summer hats which seemed to smile contentedly, followed by expensive crystal, porcelain and items of jewellery. Ali Baba enjoyed watching the pictures, each quickly dissolving and being replaced by the next.' Things are always quickly dissolving and being replaced by the next in Walser. His scenes only last for the blink of an eye, and even the human figures in his work enjoy only the briefest of lives. Hundreds of them inhabit the *Bleistiftgebiet* alone – dancers and singers, tragedians and comedians, barmaids and private tutors, principals and procurers, Nubians and Muscovites, hired hands and millionaires, Aunts

Roka and Moka and a whole host of other walk-on parts. As they make their entrance they have a marvellous presence, but as soon as one tries to look at them more closely they have already vanished. It always seems to me as if, like actors in the earliest films, they are surrounded by a trembling, shimmering aura which makes their contours unrecognizable. They flit through Walser's fragmentary stories and embryonic novels as people in dreams flit through our heads at night, never stopping to register, departing the moment they have arrived, never to be seen again. Walter Benjamin is the only one among the commentators who attempts to pin down the anonymous, evanescent quality of Walser's characters. They come, he says, 'from insanity and nowhere else. They are figures who have left madness behind them, and this is why they are marked by such a consistently heartrending, inhuman superficiality. If we were to attempt to sum up in a single phrase the delightful yet also uncanny element in them, we would have to say: they have all been healed.'[8] Nabokov surely had something similar in mind when he said of the fickle souls who roam Nikolai Gogol's books that here we have to do with a tribe of harmless madmen, who will not be prevented by anything in the world from ploughing their own eccentric furrow. The comparison with Gogol is by no means far-fetched, for if Walser had any literary relative or predecessor, then it was Gogol. Both of them gradually lost the ability to keep their eye on the centre of the plot, losing themselves instead in the almost compulsive contemplation of strangely unreal creations appearing on the periphery of their vision, about whose previous and future fate we never learn even the slightest thing. There is a scene which Nabokov quotes in his book on Gogol, where we are told that the hero of *Dead Souls*, our Mr Chichikov, is boring a certain young lady in a ballroom with all kinds of pleasantries which he had already uttered on numerous occasions in various places, for example: 'In the Government of Simbirsk, at the house of Sofron Ivanovich Bezpechnoy, where the latter's daughter, Adelaida Sofronovna, was also present with her three sisters-in-law, Maria Gavrilovna, Alexandra Gavrilovna and Adelheida Gavrilovna; at the house of Frol Vasilievich Pobedonosnoy, in the Government of Penza; and at that of the latter's brother, where the following were present: his wife's sister Katherina Mikhailovna and her cousins Rosa Feodorovna and Emilia Feodorovna; in the Government of Viatka, at the house of Pyotr Varsonophyevich, where his daughter-in-law's sister Pelagea Egorovna was present, together with a niece, Sophia Rotislavna and two stepsisters: Sophia Alexandrovna and Maclatura Alexandrovna'[9] – this scene, none of whose characters makes an appearance anywhere else in Gogol's work, since their secret (like that of human existence as a whole) resides in their utter superfluity – this scene with its digressive nature could equally well have sprung from Robert Walser's imagination. Walser himself once said that basically he was always writing the same novel, from one prose work to the next – a novel which, he says, one could describe as 'a much-chopped up or dismembered Book of Myself'. One should add that the main character – the *Ich* or 'I' – almost never makes an appearance in this *Ich-Buch* but is left blank, or rather remains out of sight among the throng of other passing figures. Homelessness is another thing Walser and Gogol have in common – the awful provisionality of their respective existences, the prismatic mood swings, the sense of panic, the wonderfully capricious humour steeped at the same time in blackest heartache, the endless scraps of paper and, of course, the invention of a whole populace of lost souls, a ceaseless masquerade for the purpose of autobiographical mystification. Just as, at the end of the spectral story *The Overcoat*, there is scarcely anything left of the scribe Akakiy Akakievich because, as Nabokov points out, he no longer quite knows if he is in the middle of the street or in the middle of a sentence, so too in the end it becomes almost impossible to make out Gogol and Walser among the legions of their characters, not to mention against the dark horizon of their looming illness. It is through writing that they achieved this depersonalization, through writing that they cut themselves off from the past. Their ideal state is that of pure amnesia. Benjamin noted that the point of every one of Walser's sentences is to make the reader forget the previous one, and indeed after *The Tanners* — which is still a family memoir — the stream of memory slows to a trickle and peters out in a sea of oblivion. For this reason it is particularly memorable, and touching, when once in a while, in some context or another, Walser raises his eyes from the page, looks back into the past and imparts to his reader — for example — that one evening years ago he was caught in a snowstorm on the Friedrichstrasse in Berlin and how the vividness of the memory has stayed with him ever since. Nor are Walser's emotions any less erratic than these remembered images. For the most part they are carefully concealed, or, if they do emerge, are soon turned into something faintly ridiculous, or at least made light of. In the prose sketch devoted to Brentano, Walser asks: 'Can a person whose feelings are so many and so lovely be at the same time so unfeeling?' The answer might have been that in life, as in fairytales, there are those who, out of fear and poverty, cannot afford emotions, and who therefore, like Walser in one of his most poignant prose pieces, have to try out their seemingly atrophied ability to love on inanimate substances and objects unheeded by anyone else – such as ash, a needle, a pencil, or a matchstick. Yet the way in which Walser then breathes life into them, in an act of complete assimilation and empathy, reveals how in the end emotions are perhaps most deeply felt when applied to the most insignificant things. 'Indeed,' Walser writes about ash, 'if one goes into this apparently uninteresting subject in any depth there is quite a lot to be said about it which is not at all uninteresting; if, for example, one blows on ash it displays not the least reluctance to fly off instantly in all directions. Ash is submissiveness, worthlessness, irrelevance itself, and best of all, it is itself pervaded by the belief that it is fit for nothing. Is it possible to be more helpless, more impotent, and more wretched than ash? Not very easily. Could anything be more compliant and more tolerant? Hardly. Ash has no notion of character and is further from any kind of wood than dejection is from exhilaration. Where there is ash there is actually nothing at all. Tread on ash, and you will barely notice that you have stepped on anything.' The intense pathos of this passage – there is nothing which comes near it in the whole of twentieth-century German literature, not even in Kafka – lies in the fact that here, in this apparently casual treatise on ash, needle, pencil and matchstick, the author is in truth writing about his own martyrdom, for these four objects are not randomly strung together but are the writer's own instruments of torture, or at any rate those which he needs in order to stage his own personal auto-da-fé – and what remains once the fire has died down.

Indeed, by the middle of his life writing had become a wearisome business for Walser. Year by year the unremitting composition of his literary pieces becomes harder and harder for him. It is a kind of penance he is serving up there in his attic room in the Hotel zum Blauen Kreuz, where, by his own account, he spends ten to thirteen hours at a stretch at his desk every day, in winter wearing his army greatcoat and the slippers he has fashioned himself from leftover scraps of material. He talks in terms of a writer's prison, a dungeon, or an attic cell,[10] and of the danger of losing one's reason under the relentless strain of composition. 'My back is bent by it,' says the Poet in the eponymous piece, 'since often I sit for hours bent over a single word that has to take the long slow route from brain to paper.' This work makes him neither unhappy nor happy, he adds, but he often has the feeling that it will be the death of him. There are several reasons – apart from the chains which, in the main, double-bind writers to their métier – why, despite these insights, Walser did not give up writing earlier: chief among them perhaps the fear of *déclassement* and, in the most extreme case in which he almost found himself, of being reduced to handouts, fears which haunted him all the more since his father's financial ruin had rendered his childhood and youth deeply insecure. It is not so much poverty itself Walser fears, however, as the ignominy of going down in the world. He is very well aware of the fact that 'a penniless worker is much less an object of contempt than an out-of-work clerk . . . A clerk, as long as he has a post, is already halfway to being a gentleman, but without a post becomes an awkward, superfluous, burdensome nonentity.' And what is true of office clerks naturally applies to an even greater degree to writers, inasmuch as the latter have it in them not just to be halfway to a gentleman but even, given the right circumstances, to rise to be figureheads of their nation. And then there is the fact that writers, in common with all those to whom a higher office is entrusted as it were by the grace of God, cannot simply retire when the mood takes them; even today they are expected to keep writing until the pen drops from their hand. Not only that: people believe they are entitled to expect that, as Walser writes to Otto Pick, 'every year they will bring to the light of day some new one hundred per cent proof item'. To bring such pieces of 'one hundred per cent proof' – in the sense of a sensational major new work – to the cultural market-place was something which Walser, at least since his return to Switzerland, was no longer in a fit state to do – if indeed he ever had been. At least part of him perceived himself, in his time in Biel or Berne, as a hired hand and as nothing more than a degraded literary haberdasher. The courage, however, with which he defended this last embattled position and came to terms with 'the disappointments, reprimands in the press, the boos and hisses, the silencing even unto the grave' was almost unprecedented. That in the end he was still forced to capitulate was due not only to the exhaustion of his own inner resources, but also to the catastrophic changes – even more rapid in the second half of the 1920s – in the cultural and intellectual climate. There can be no doubt that had Walser persevered for a few more years he would, by the spring of 1933 at the latest, have found the last possible opportunities for publication in the German Reich closed off to him. To that extent, he was quite correct in the remarks he made to Carl Seelig that his world had been destroyed by the Nazis. In his 1908 critical review of *Der Gehülfe* [*The Assistant*], Josef Hofmiller contrasts the alleged insubstantiality of the novel with the more solid earthiness of the autochthonous Swiss writers Johannes Jegerlehner, Josef Reinhart, Alfred Huggenberger, Otto von Greyerz and Ernst Zahn – whose ideological slant may, I make so bold as to claim, be readily discerned from the ingrained rootedness of their names. Of one such *Heimat* poet, a certain Hans von Mühlenstein, Walser writes in the mid 1920s to Resy Breitbach that he – like Walser himself originally from Biel – after a brief marriage to an imposing lady from Munich has now settled in Graubünden, where he is an active member of the association for the dissemination of the new spirit of the age and has married a country woman 'who orders him first thing in the morning to bring in a cartload of greens from the field before breakfast. He wears a blue linen smock, with coarse trousers of a rustic stuff, and is exceedingly contented.' The contempt for nationalistic and *Heimat* poets which this passage reveals is a clear indication that Walser knew exactly what ill hour had struck and why there was no longer any call for his works, either in Germany or at home in Switzerland.

Against this background, Walser's legendary 'pencil system' takes on the aspect of preparation for a life underground. In the

Sepia photograph of the Kleist house
on the island in the River Aare

'microscripts', the deciphering of which by Werner Morlang and Bernhard Echte is one of the most significant literary achievements of recent decades, can be seen – as an ingenious method of continuing to write – the coded messages of one forced into illegitimacy, and documents of a genuine 'inner emigration'. Certainly Walser was, as he explains in a letter to Max Rychner, primarily concerned with overcoming his inhibitions about writing by means of the less definitive 'pencil method'; and it is equally certain that unconsciously, as Werner Morlang notes, he was seeking to hide, behind the indecipherable characters, 'from both public and internalized instances of evaluation', to duck down below the level of language and to obliterate himself. But his system of pencil notes on scraps of paper is also a work of fortifications and defences, unique in the history of literature, by means of which the smallest and most innocent things might be saved from destruction in the 'great times' then looming on the horizon. Entrenched in his impenetrable earthworks, Robert Walser reminds me of Casella, the Corsican captain who, in 1768, alone in a tower on Cap Corse, deceived the French invaders into believing it was occupied by a whole battalion by running from one floor to another and shooting now out of one, now out of another firing slit. Significantly enough, after Walser entered the asylum at Waldau he felt as if he were perched outside the city on the ramparts, and it is perhaps for this reason that he writes from there to Fräulein Breitbach that, although the battle has long since been lost, now and again he 'fires off' the odd small piece at 'some of the journals of the *Vaterland*', just as if these writings were grenades or incendiary bombs. At any rate I am

unable to reassure myself with the view that the intricate texts of the *Bleistiftgebiet* reflect, in either their appearance or their content, the history of Robert Walser's progressive mental deterioration. I recognize, of course, that their peculiar preoccupation with form, the extreme compulsion to rhyme, say, or the way that their length is determined by the exact dimensions of the space available on a scrap of paper, exhibit certain characteristics

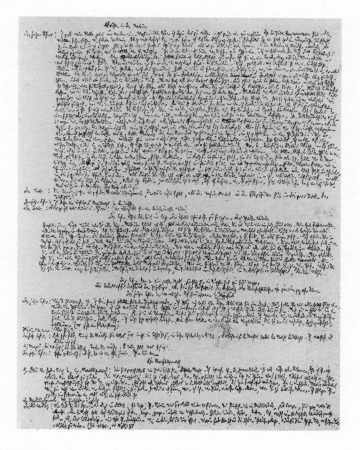

of pathological writing: an encephalogram, as it were, of someone compelled – as it says in *The Robber* – to be thinking constantly
of something somehow very far distant; but they do not appear
to me to be evidence of a psychotic state. On the contrary, *Der
Räuber* is Walser's most rational and most daring work, a self-
portrait and self-examination of absolute integrity, in which both
the compiler of the medical history and his subject occupy the

position of the author. Accordingly, the narrator – who is at once friend, attorney, warden, guardian and guardian angel of the vulnerable, almost broken hero – sets out his case from a certain ironic distance, even perhaps, as he notes on one occasion, with the complacency of a critic. On the other hand he repeatedly rises to the occasion with impassioned pleas on behalf of his client, such as in the following appeal to the public: 'Don't persist in reading nothing but healthy books, acquaint yourselves also with so-called pathological literature, from which you may derive considerable edification. Healthy people should always, so to speak, take certain risks. For what other reason, blast and confound it, is a person healthy? Simply in order to stop living one day at the height of one's health? A damned bleak fate . . . I know now more than ever that intellectual circles are filled with philistinism. I mean moral and aesthetic chicken-heartedness. Timidity, though, is unhealthy. One day, while out for a swim, the Robber very nearly met a watery end . . . One year later, that dairy school student drowned in the very same river. So the Robber knows from experience what it's like to have water nymphs hauling one down by the legs.' The passion with which the advocate Walser takes up the cause on his client's behalf draws its energy from the threat of annihilation. If ever a book was written from the outermost brink, it is this one. Faced with the imminent end, Walser works imperturbably on, often even with a kind of wry amusement, and – apart from a few eccentricities which he permits himself for the fun of it – with an unerringly steady hand. 'Never before, in all my years at my desk, have I sat down to write so boldly, so intrepidly,' the narrator tells us at the beginning. In fact, the unforced way in which he manages the not inconsiderable structural difficulties and the constant switches of mood between the deepest distraction and a light-heartedness which can only be properly described by the word *allegría*, testifies to a supreme degree of both aesthetic and moral assurance. It is true, too, that in this posthumous novel – already written, so to speak, from the other side – Walser accrues insights into his own particular state of mind and the nature of mental disturbance as such, the likes of which, so far as I can see, are to be found nowhere else in literature. With incomparable sangfroid he sets down an account of the probable origins of his suffering in an upbringing which consisted almost exclusively of small acts of neglect; of how, as a man of fifty, he still feels the child or little boy inside him; of the girl he would like to have been; the satisfaction he derives from wearing an apron; the fetishistic tendencies of the spoon-caresser; of paranoia, the feeling of being surrounded and hemmed in; the sense, reminiscent of Josef K. in *The Trial*, that being observed made him interesting; and of the dangers of idiocy arising, as he actually writes, from sexual atrophy. With seismographic precision he registers the slightest tremors at the edges of his consciousness, records rejections and ripples in his thoughts and emotions of which the science of psychiatry even today scarcely allows itself to dream. The narrator does not think much of the therapies the mind doctor offers to the Robber, and still less of the universal panacea of belief, which he terms a 'perfectly simple, paltry condition of the soul'. 'For,' he says, 'one achieves nothing by it, absolutely nothing, nothing at all. One just sits there and believes. Like a person mechanically knitting a sock.' Walser is not interested in either the obscurantism of the medicine men or of the other curators of the soul. What matters to him, like any other writer in full possession of his faculties, is the greatest possible degree of lucidity, and I can imagine how, while writing *Der Raüber*, it must have occurred to him on more than one occasion that the looming threat of impending darkness enabled him at times to arrive at an acuity of observation and precision of formulation which is unattainable from a state of perfect health. He focuses this particular power of perception not just on his own *via dolorosa* but also on other outsiders, persons excluded and eliminated, with whom his alter ego the Robber is associated. His own personal fate concerns him least of all. 'In most people,' the narrator says, 'the lights go out,' and he feels for every such ravaged life. The French officers, for example, whom the Robber once saw in mufti in the resort town of Magglingen, 3,000 feet above sea level. 'This was shortly before the outbreak of our not yet forgotten Great War, and all these young gentlemen who sought and doubtless also found relaxation high up in the blossoming meads were obliged to follow the call of their nation.' How false, then, the rolling thunder of 'storms of steel'[11] and all ideologically tainted literature sounds, by comparison with this one sentence with its discreet compassion. Walser refused the grand gesture. On the subject of the collective catastrophes of his day he remained resolutely silent. However, he was anything but politically naïve. When, in the years preceding the First World War, the old Ottoman Empire collapsed in the face of attacks by the reform party, and modern Turkey constituted itself with one eye on Germany as a potential

protector, Walser was more or less alone in viewing this development with scepticism. In the prose piece 'The Farewell' ['Abschied']
he has the deposed Sultan – who is under no illusions about the
shortcomings of his regime – express doubts about the progress
that has apparently been achieved. Of course, he says, there will
now be efficient folk at work in Turkey, where chaos has always
reigned, 'but our gardens will wither and our mosques will soon
be redundant . . . [and] railways will criss-cross the desert where
even hyenas quailed at the sound of my name. The Turks will put
on caps and look like Germans. We will be forced to engage in
commerce, and if we aren't capable of that, we will simply be
shot.' That is more or less how things came to pass, too, except
that in the first genocide of our ill-fated century it was not the
Turks who were shot and put to death by the Germans, but the
Armenians by the Turks. At all events, it was hardly an auspicious
start, and one could say that in 1909, looking through the eyes
of Haroun al Rashid, Walser saw far into the future; and he will
hardly have been less far-sighted as the 1920s drew to a close.
The Robber, whose whole disposition was that of a liberal free-
thinker and republican, *also* became soul-sick on account of the
looming clouds darkening the political horizon. The exact diag-
nosis of his illness is of little relevance. It is enough for us to
understand that, in the end, Walser simply could not go on, and,
like Hölderlin, had to resort to keeping people at arm's length
with a sort of anarchic politeness, becoming refractory and
abusive, making scenes in public and believing that the bourgeois
city of Berne, of all places, was a city of ghostly gesticulators,
executing rapid hand movements directly in front of his face

expressly in order to discombobulate him and to dismiss him out of hand as one who simply does not count. During his years in Berne, Walser was almost completely isolated. The contempt was, as he feared, universal. Among the few who still concerned themselves with him was the schoolteacher (and poet) Emil Schibli, with whom he stayed for a few days in 1927. In a description of his meeting with Walser published in the *Seeländer Volksstimme*, Schibli claims to have recognized, in this lonely poet in the guise of a tramp and suffering from profound isolation, a king in hiding 'whom posterity will call, if not one of the great, then one of rare purity'. While Walser was no stranger to the evangelical desire to possess nothing and to give away everything one owns – as in *The Robber* – he made no claim to any kind of messianic calling. It was enough for him to call himself – with bitterly resigned irony – at least the ninth-best writer in the Helvetic Federation. We, though, can grant Walser the honorific title with which he endows the Robber and to which in fact he himself is entitled, namely the son of a first secretary to the canton.

The first prose work I read by Robert Walser was his piece on Kleist in Thun, where he talks of the torment of one despairing of himself and his craft, and of the intoxicating beauty of the surrounding landscape. 'Kleist sits on a churchyard wall. Everything is damp, yet also sultry. He opens his shirt, to breathe freely. Below him lies the lake, as if it had been hurled down by the great hand of a god, incandescent with shades of yellow and red . . . The Alps have come to life and dip with fabulous gestures their foreheads in the water.' Time and again I have immersed myself in the few pages of this story and, taking it as a starting point, have undertaken now shorter, now longer excursions into the rest of Walser's work. Among my early encounters with Walser I count the discovery I made, in an antiquarian bookshop in Manchester in the second half of the 1960s – inserted in a copy of Bächtold's three-volume biography of Gottfried Keller which had almost certainly belonged to a German-Jewish refugee – of an attractive sepia photograph depicting the house on the island in the Aare, completely surrounded by shrubs and trees, in which Kleist worked on his drama of madness, *Die Familie Ghonorez*,[12] before he, himself sick, was obliged to commit himself to the care of Dr Wyttenbach in Berne. Since then I have slowly learned to grasp how everything is connected across space and time, the life of the Prussian writer Kleist with that of a Swiss author who claims to have worked as a clerk in a brewery in Thun, the echo of a pistol shot across the Wannsee with the view from a window of the Herisau asylum, Walser's long walks with my own travels, dates of birth with dates of death, happiness with misfortune, natural history and the history of our industries, that of *Heimat* with that of exile. On all these paths Walser has been my constant companion. I only need to look up for a moment in my daily work to see him standing somewhere a little apart, the unmistakable figure of the solitary walker just pausing to take in the surroundings. And sometimes I imagine that I see with his eyes the bright Seeland and within this land of lakes the lake like a shimmering island, and in this lake-island another island, the Île Saint-Pierre, 'shining in the bright morning haze, floating in a sea of pale trembling light'. Returning home then in the evening we look out, from the lakeside path suffused by mournful rain, at the boating enthusiasts out on the lake 'in boats or skiffs with umbrellas opened above their heads', a sight which allows us to imagine that we are 'in China or Japan or some other dreamlike, poetical land'. As Mächler reminds us, Walser really did consider for a while the possibility of travelling, or even emigrating, overseas. According to his brother, he once even had a cheque in his pocket from Bruno Cassirer, good for several months' travel to India. It is not difficult to imagine him hidden in a green leafy picture by Henri Rousseau, with tigers and elephants, on the veranda of a hotel by the sea while the monsoon pours down outside, or in front of a resplendent tent in the foothills of the Himalayas, which – as Walser once wrote of the Alps – resemble nothing so much as a snow-white fur boa. In fact he almost got as far as Samoa, since Walter Rathenau, whom – if we may believe *The Robber* on this point – he had met one day, quite by chance, in the midst of an incessant stream of people and traffic on the Potsdamer Platz in Berlin, apparently wanted to find him a not-too-taxing position in the colonial administration on the island known to the Germans as the 'Pearl of the South Seas'. We do not know why Walser turned down this in many ways tempting offer. Let us simply assume that it is because, among the first German South Sea discoverers and explorers, there was a certain gentleman called Otto von Kotzebue, against whom Walser was just as irrevocably prejudiced as he was against the playwright of the same name,[13] whom he called a narrow-minded philistine, claiming he had a too-long nose, bulging eyes and no neck, and that his whole head was shrunk into and hidden by a grotesque and enormous collar. Kotzebue had, so Walser continues, written a large number of comedies which enjoyed runaway box office success at a time when Kleist was in despair, and bequeathed a whole series of these massive, collected, printed volumes, coxed and boxed and bound in calf-skin, to a posterity which would blench with shame were it ever to read them. The risk of being reminded, in the midst of a South Sea idyll, of this literary opportunist, one of the heroes of the German intellectual scene, as he dismissively calls him, was probably just too great. In any case, Walser didn't much care for travel and − apart from Germany − never actually went anywhere to speak of. He never saw the city of Paris, which he dreams of even from the asylum at Waldau. On the other hand, the Untergasse in Biel could seem to him like a street in Jerusalem 'along which the Saviour and deliverer of the world modestly rides in'. Indeed he criss-crossed the country on foot, often on nocturnal route marches with the moon shining a white track before him. In the autumn of 1925, for example, he journeyed on foot from Berne to Geneva, following for quite a long stretch the old pilgrim route to Santiago de Compostela. He does not tell us much about this trip, other than that in Fribourg − I can see him entering that city across the incredibly high bridge over the Sarine − he purchased some socks; paid his respects to a number of hostelries; whispered sweet nothings to a waitress from the Jura; gave a boy almonds; strolling around in the dark doffed his hat to the Rousseau monument on the island in the Rhône; and, crossing the bridges by the lake, experienced a feeling of light-heartedness. Such and similar matters are set down for us in the most economical manner on a couple of pages. Of the walk itself, we learn nothing and nothing about what he may have pondered in his mind as he walked. The only occasion on which I see the traveller Robert Walser freed from the burden of himself is on the balloon journey he undertook, during his Berlin years, from Bitterfeld – the artificial lights of whose factories were just beginning to glimmer – to the Baltic coast. 'Three people, the captain, a gentleman, and a young girl, climb into the basket, the anchoring cords are loosed, and the strange house flies, slowly, as if it had first to ponder something, upward . . . The beautiful moonlit night seems to gather the splendid balloon into invisible arms, gently and quietly the roundish flying body ascends, and . . . hardly so that one might notice, subtle winds propel it northward.' Far below can be seen church spires, village schools, farmyards, a ghostly train whistling by, the wonderfully illuminated course of the Elbe in all its colours. 'Remarkably white, polished-looking plains alternate with gardens and small wildernesses of bush. One peers down into regions where one's feet would never, never have trod, because in certain regions, indeed in most, one has no purpose whatever. How big and unknown to us the earth is!' Robert Walser was, I think, born for just such a silent journey through the air. In all his prose works he always seeks to rise above the heaviness of earthly existence, wanting to float away softly and silently into a higher, freer realm. The sketch about the balloon journey over a sleeping nocturnal Germany is only one example, one which for me is associated with Nabokov's memory of one of his favourite books from his childhood. In this picture-book series, the black Golliwog and his friends – one of whom is a kind of dwarf or Lilliputian person – survive a number of adventures, end up far away from home and are even captured by cannibals. And then

there is a scene where an airship is made of 'yards and yards of yellow silk . . . and an additional tiny balloon . . . provided for the sole use of the fortunate Midget. At the immense altitude,' writes Nabokov, 'to which the ship reached, the aeronauts huddled together for warmth while the lost little soloist, still the object of my intense envy notwithstanding his plight, drifted into an abyss of frost and stars – alone.'[14]

As Day and Night . . .

On the paintings of Jan Peter Tripp

Grapes II, Jan Peter Tripp, 1988

The catalogue of Jan Peter Tripp's oeuvre today goes back over a quarter of a century. It comprises works on a range of vastly differing scales, executed in pencil, charcoal and drypoint, in watercolour, gouache and *grisaille*, acrylics and oil, taken to the furthest limit of the possible and frequently, or so it appears to the observer, some way beyond it. The pictures from the first three or four years of Tripp's career still clearly show the influence of surrealism, of the Vienna school of fantastic realists, and of photorealism, still embedded in the polemical strategies of 1968; but soon afterwards, during the months spent as an artist in the regional psychiatric hospital at Weissenau near Ravensburg in 1973, this polemical trait disappears, to be replaced by a far more radical objectivity which, by simply representing life in all its manifestations, seeks to establish what gives rise to its particular evolution and expression. In this way, the art of portraiture becomes an exercise in pathography, no longer admitting of any distinction between what is generally known as the character of the individual and the deformations occasioned by the ordeals of work and mental suffering in the subject portrayed. If the paintings of the Weissenau asylum inmates may be understood as studies of the echoing void in the heads of humankind, then this is no less true of the late portraits and self-portraits, with their almost other-worldly sense of isolation. Even the most recent portraits of respected incumbents of positions of economic and political power have (without the slightest defamatory intention) a tortured self-consciousness and a slight air of derangement

about them, and so share a secret affinity with the definition, arrived at in Weissenau, of the human individual as an aberrant creature, forcibly removed from its natural and social environment. The obverse of this depiction, of a race growing ever more monstrous in the so-called process of civilization, are the deserted landscapes, devoid of all human presence, and in particular the still lifes, in which, far removed from the world of events, only the motionless objects are left to bear witness to the former presence of a strangely rationalistic species. Tripp's still lifes are not primarily concerned with the skill and mastery of the artist, exercised upon a more or less random *assemblage*, but rather with the autonomous life of things – in relation to which we, as creatures in blind thrall to the world of work, find ourselves in a subordinate and dependent position. Since (in theory) things outlast us, they know more about us than we do about them; they bear their experience of us within them and *are* – in a literal sense – the book of our history lying open before us. In the father's so-called Russian suitcase

lie the shoes of the son; two dozen slates and a few faded scribblings evoke an entire vanished class of schoolchildren – images of the past, of the most mysterious aspects of a life. In Tripp's work, more clearly than ever before, the *nature morte* represents the paradigmatic expression of what we leave behind. Looking at it, we become aware of what Maurice Merleau-Ponty, in *L'Œil et l'Esprit*, has called 'le regard préhumain', for in such painting the role of the observer and the observed object are reversed. In gazing, the painter surrenders our all-too-superficial knowledge; things look across at us, unblinking, and fix us in their gaze. 'Action et passion si peu discernables,' writes Merleau-Ponty, 'qu'on ne sait plus qui voit et qui est vu, qui peint et qui est peint.'[1]

Thinking about the work of Jan Peter Tripp, and the way in which, in it, the exact reproduction of reality achieves an almost unimaginable degree of precision, it is impossible to avoid the tiresome question of realism. On the one hand, because the first thing to strike anyone looking at a picture by Tripp is the apparently flawless accuracy of representation, and on the other because, paradoxically, it is precisely this astounding facility which distorts the view of its true achievement. The perfect surface of the completed picture offers so little in the way of clues that even professional art criticism has scarcely anything meaningful to add to the lay utterances of astonished admiration. Such utterances are, moreover, typically made with (so to speak) an incredulous shake of the head, since the unquestioning admiration is in all likelihood tempered – particularly in the case of those critics schooled in the traditions of modernism, who tend on the whole to be largely ignorant when it comes to matters of technique – with the uneasy sensation of having been taken in by some kind of illusionist or confidence trickster operating with all manner of inscrutable sleights of hand. Indeed, not only does Tripp succeed in interpolating the third dimension into the surface of the painting, to the extent that, looking at it, one sometimes has the feeling one could step over the threshold and enter the picture itself; but the materials represented, too, the cypress-black of young Marcel's velveteen jacket, his taffeta bow, the forty-one pebbles, and the white snow on the field, appear so truly *real* in the painting that one involuntarily reaches out a hand to touch

it. Ernst Gombrich, in his comprehensive work on art and illusion, recalls the story Pliny relates of the two Greek painters Parrhasius and Zeuxis.[2] Zeuxis, it is said, painted grapes in such a deceptively realistic manner that the birds tried to peck at them. Parrhasius then invited Zeuxis to his studio in order to show him his own work. When Zeuxis went to draw back the curtain in front of the picture to which Parrhasius led him, he discovered that it was not in fact real, but only painted. Gombrich goes on to explain how, in *trompe l'oeil* painting, the suggestive power of the picture and the expectation on the part of the viewer mutually reinforce each other, and he concludes the section with the remark that the most convincing *trompe l'oeil* he had ever seen 'simulated' a broken pane of glass in front of the picture.[3] Well, in Tripp's work we find both the grapes of Zeuxis and the broken pane of glass. And yet it would be wrong to regard him first and

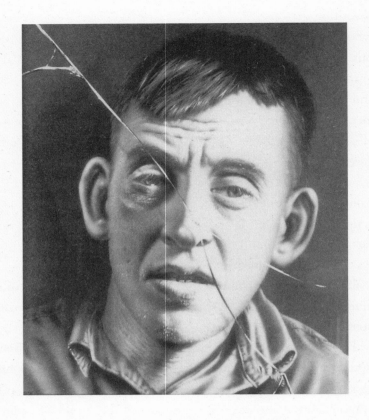

foremost as a virtuoso of *trompe l'oeil* painting. Tripp makes use of *trompe l'oeil* as just one technique among many, and always – as the watercolour *Ein leiser Sprung* [*A Little Crack(ed)*] illustrates – with the closest possible link to the subject of the painting.

Trompe l'oeil is a manner of painting capable, with relatively limited means – whether by a certain organization of perspective, or an astute deployment of light and shade – of conjuring up the so-called *effet du réel* as it were from nothing. Its most adept practitioners were, of course, the *quadratisti* of the baroque era, who travelled all over Austria and Bavaria conferring upon various not particularly impressive *intérieurs* an illusion of palatial grandeur by painting the walls with whole series of colonnades, and grandiose domes on the ceilings. The whiff of trickery and inconsequentiality, which attaches to any artistic practice whose effects can be indiscriminately deployed, later – at least since the dawn of photography and the beginnings of the modernist era which it ushers in – came to be extended to representational painting as a whole. For this reason, the idea that radically exposed artistic positions might nowadays be arrived at just as readily through representational as non-representational art is, for an art critic, virtually inconceivable; the more so as photo- or hyper-realism, with the tendency to reification implicit in its naturalistic mode of depiction, very rapidly arrived at the limit of its artistic possibilities.

That Tripp's work is – almost inevitably – discussed in connection with this virtually outmoded movement is, then, the result of a false association. The one thing which seems to me worthy of note is the – implicit – suggestion that the essence of a painting by Jan Peter Tripp lies not in what one might assume to be the purely objective and affirmatory quality of its identical reproduction of reality (or the latter's photographic image) – that quality which is without fail admired by each and every viewer – but rather in the far more subtle ways in which it deviates and differs from it. The photographic image makes a tautology of reality. When Cartier-Bresson goes to China, writes Susan Sontag, he shows that there are people in China and that these people are

Chinese. What may be true of photography, though, is not necessarily applicable to art. The latter depends on ambiguity, polyvalence, resonance, obfuscation and illumination, in short, the transcending of that which, according to an ineluctable law, has necessarily to be the case. Roland Barthes saw in the – now omnipresent – man with a camera an agent of death, and in photographs something like the relics of life continually giving way to death. Where art differs from such a morbid affair is in the fact that the proximity of life to death is its subject, not its obsession. Art deploys the deconstruction of outward appearances as a means of countering the obliteration, in endless series of reproductions, of the visible world. Accordingly, Jan Peter Tripp's paintings, too, have a consistently analytic quality rather than a synthesizing one. The photographic raw material which they take as their starting point is painstakingly modified. Artificial distinctions between focus and out-of-focus effects are dissolved; additions and subtractions made. Something may be moved to another place, foreshortened, or rotated a fraction out of kilter. Tonal shades are altered, and from time to time those happy accidents occur which unexpectedly give rise to a system of representation directly opposed to reality. Without such interventions, deviations and differences, the most perfect re-presentation would be devoid of all thought or feeling. What is more, looking at Tripp's pictures one would do well to bear in mind Gombrich's lapidary statement that even the most meticulous realist can accommodate only a limited number of marks in the allotted space. 'And though he may try,' writes Gombrich, 'to smooth out the transition between his dabs of paint beyond the threshold of visibility, in the end he will always have to rely on suggestion when it comes to representing the infinitely small. While standing in front of a painting by Jan van Eyck we . . . believe he succeeded in rendering the inexhaustible wealth of detail that belongs to the visible world. We have the impression that he painted every stitch of the golden damask, every hair of the angels, every fibre of the wood. Yet he clearly could not have done that, however patiently he worked with a magnifying glass.'[4] In other words, the creation of a perfect illusion depends not only upon a vertiginous degree of technical ability, but ultimately upon the intuitive channelling of a breathless state in which the painter himself no longer knows whether his eye still sees or his hand still moves.

The recurring experience of a state of utmost concentration in which the breath grows ever shallower, the silence ever greater, the limbs gradually grow numb and the eyes grow dim brought death into the paintings of Jan Peter Tripp. Unmistakably present in the early studies of bones and skulls, in later works it tends to lie concealed within the ominous-looking objects, in the faces of those portrayed, in the crack in the glass, the hermetic form of the pebbles, or the portrait of Kafka at fifty. In order to discover it, the painter had to venture across the border. On the way to the other side, too, was the dormouse discovered one morning lying on the doorstep. Although it is said that one should paint the dead quickly, surrounded by the chloroform stench of decomposition Tripp took seven days over the picture in which the silent message of this unexpected guest is preserved. On the seventh day, there was one final tiny movement in the long-since lifeless

body, and a drop of blood the size of a pinhead appeared at the nostril. That was the true end. Nestling in nothingness, with neither ground nor background, the creature hovers now, its bat ears extended, through thin air. The black patch of fur around its eyes is reminiscent of a mourning band, or an eye mask worn by a sleeping passenger on a summer night's flight over the North Pole. *We are such stuff / as dreams are made on; and our little life / is rounded with a sleep.*[5]

The longer I look at the paintings of Jan Peter Tripp, the more I realize that beneath the surface illusionism there lurks a terrifying abyss. It is, so to speak, the metaphysical underside of reality, its dark inner lining. This hidden lining is revealed in a series of flower paintings, only recently begun, which despite their high degree of realism leave botanical illustration far behind. The flowers, which originally were to have been painted in the full glory of their natural colours, have become silent *grisailles* in which only the ghostliest trace of colour remains. They are as if disembodied, trapped in the porcelain stillness of death. All of them bear women's names, and as such are of another kind. Yet their flamboyant, diva-like forms still retain a pale reflection, faded almost to nothing, of organic living nature. In the painting of the green grapes, too, these latter represent one last sign of life. A strangely ceremonial, emblematic style governs the composition. The dark background, the white linen cloth with the embroidered monogram – already we begin to sense that it is spread out not for a wedding breakfast, but on a bier or cata-falque. And what is the business of painting in any case but a kind of pathological investigation in the face of the blackness of death and the white light of eternity? This extreme contrast of light and dark recurs on a number of occasions, for example in the cheq-uerboard pattern of the floor tiles in the Belgian billiard picture

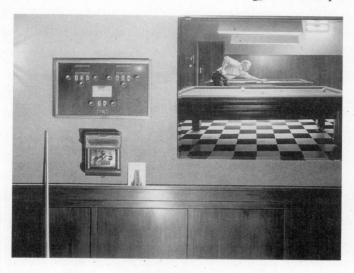

from Tongres, which not coincidentally seems to suggest that in any given frame the painter is embarking upon a game of chance in which one false move risks losing everything. In one of Tripp's earliest paintings, the 'kobaltblaue Krapplackkugel' [cobalt blue madder ball] is already rolling away towards a nocturnal vanishing point on the other side, and, in each of the pictures that follow, the most intricate chess moves, circumventions and evasions are played out back and forth between life and death: *'tis all a Chequerboard of Nights and Days / Where Destiny with Men for Pieces plays / Hither and thither moves, and mates, and slays / And one by one, back in the Closet lays.*[6]

Closely bound up with the theme of death is that of time passing, time past and lost time, which in Jan Peter Tripp's pictures is suspended — just as in Proust — as ephemeral moments and constellations are preserved from the passage of time. A red glove, a burnt-out match, a pearl onion on a chopping board: these objects contain the whole of time within themselves, as it were redeemed for ever by the painstaking, impassioned precision of the artist's work. The aura of memory which surrounds them lends them the quality of mementos: objects in which melancholy is crystallized. An interior from La Cadière d'Azur

shows a whitewashed wall and the corner of a reproduction in oils, black with age, on which it is just possible to make out the motif of a boating trip across the water. On the wide plaster frame of the print – disguised to look like a mount – is fastened a miniature painted on ivory, a bust in the truest sense of the word, since the face of the subject is so scratched away as to be unrecognizable, and only the head and blue-uniformed shoulders of the unknown hero can be seen. Also attached to the frame is a small bunch of dried flowers (it immediately reminded me of the garland which Karoline von Schlieben wove with Heinrich von Kleist on the Brühlsche Terrasse in Dresden on the 16th of May 1801, a photograph of which has survived), as well as a scrap of paper torn from a diary bearing the date of the 15th of May – the painter's birthday.

Time lost, the pain of remembering, and the figure of death are here assembled like mementos in a shrine to remembrance, quotations from the painter's own life. Remembrance, after all, is in the end nothing other than a quotation. And the quotation interpolated into a text or an image forces us, as Eco writes, to revisit what we know of other texts and images, and reconsider our knowledge of the world. That, in turn, requires time. In taking it, we enter upon narrated time and cultural time. Let us attempt, by way of conclusion, to demonstrate this with the help of the painting entitled *La Déclaration de guerre*, measuring 370 x 220 cm, in which an elegant pair of ladies' shoes is to be seen upon a tiled floor. The pale-blue and off-white pattern on the tiles, the grey lines of the grouting, the diamond pattern cast by the leaded light of the window across the central portion of the

picture, in which the black shoes stand between two areas of shadow; all this taken together produces a geometric pattern of a complexity which is incapable of expression in words. From a combination of this pattern – illustrating the intricacy of the various proportions, relationships and interlocking connections – and the mysterious pair of black shoes, there arises a kind of picture puzzle which the observer, knowing nothing of the previous history, will scarcely be able to solve. Who was the woman the shoes belonged to? Where has she gone? Do the shoes now belong to someone else? Or are they, in the end, simply a paradigm for the fetish which the painter is compelled to make of everything he paints? It is difficult to say more about this picture than that, notwithstanding its imposing scale and deceptive simplicity, it remains locked in the most intimate private sphere. The shoes give nothing away. Two years later, however, the painter brings his enigmatic picture at least a little further into the open. In a work of significantly smaller format (100 x 145 cm), the large picture reappears, not just as a quotation but as a mediating element of the painting. Filling the upper two thirds of the canvas, it is evidently now hanging in its rightful place, and in front of it, in front of the *Déclaration de guerre*, perched sideways on a mahogany chair with white upholstery, a woman with flaming-red hair sits with her back to the observer. She is smartly dressed, but still gives the appearance of someone weary at evening from the burdens of the day. She has removed one of her shoes – the same shoes as the ones she is gazing at in the large picture. Originally, so I have been told, she was holding this one shoe in her left hand, then it was placed on the floor to

the right of the chair, and finally it vanished altogether. The woman wearing one shoe, alone with the mysterious declaration of war – alone, that is, apart from the faithful dog at her side, who, however, is not in the least interested in the painted shoes, but gazes straight ahead out of the picture and looks us directly in the eye. An X-ray would show that previously he was standing in the middle of the picture. In the meantime, he has been on a journey, and has retrieved a kind of wooden sandal from the fifteenth century, or, as the case may be, from the wedding portrait which hangs in the National Gallery in London, painted by Jan van Eyck in 1434 for Giovanni Arnolfini and his wife in morganatic 'left-handed' marriage, Giovanna Cenami, in token of his witness to the union. *Johannes de Eyck hic fuit,* it says on

the frame of the circular mirror in which the scene can be seen again, in miniature, from behind. In the foreground, near the bottom-left-hand edge of the painting, lies the wooden sandal – that strange piece of evidence – next to a small dog who has somehow got into the picture, probably as a symbol of marital fidelity. The red-haired woman, who in Jan Peter Tripp's painting is meditating on the fate of her shoes and an inexplicable loss, has no idea that the revelation of the secret lies behind her – in the form of an analogous object from a world long since past. The dog, bearer of secrets who leaps easily over the dark abysses of time, because for him there is no difference between the fifteenth and the twentieth centuries, knows many things better than we. His left (domesticated) eye looks straight at us; the

right (untamed) eye has just a shade less light, seems remote
and strange. And yet, we feel, it is precisely this eye in shadow
which can see right through us.

Translator's Notes

In the 'extended marginal notes and glosses' — as he modestly characterizes the essays in *A Place in the Country* — W. G. Sebald chooses to dispense with the usual scholarly accoutrements of footnotes (with a single exception) and Bibliography. In reintroducing such apparatus as an aid for the English reader, I have accordingly tried to keep these notes as unobtrusive as possible, refraining from footnoting the numerous embedded quotations, half-quotations and allusions. Instead, works cited in the text are, as far as possible, listed and referenced in the Bibliography, where details of the English translations of the authors in question, to which my own translation is indebted, may be found.

Foreword

1. The phrase 'Aufzählen der Dinge' (recounting or recollection of things) would seem to be a reference to the title of the 1993 catalogue of Jan Peter Tripp's work in which this essay was first published: Jan Peter Tripp, *Die Aufzählung der Schwierigkeiten. Arbeiten von 1985–92* (Offenburg: Reiff-Schwarzwaldverlag, 1993). Part of the essay on Robert Walser appeared in the *Neue Zürcher*

Zeitung on 23 May 1998. The essay on Mörike was given as an acceptance speech for the Mörike Prize in Fellbach (near Stuttgart) on 22 April 1997 (see *Mörike-Preis der Stadt Fellbach: Ein Lesebuch 1991–2000* (Fellbach, 2000)), while the essay on Rousseau was first published, with minor variants, under the title 'Rousseau auf der Île de Saint-Pierre' in *Sinn und Form* 50.4 (July–August 1998); neither of these last includes any images.

A Comet in the Heavens

1. Walter Benjamin, 'Johann Peter Hebel (I): On the Centenary of His Death', English translation by Rodney Livingstone, in Walter Benjamin: *Selected Writings 1913–1926*, vol. 1, eds. Marcus Bullock and Michael W. Jennings (Cambridge, Mass.: Belknap Press of Harvard University Press, 1996) (*Gesammelte Schriften*, vol. II.i, eds. Rolf Tiedemann and Hermann Schweppenhäuser, pp. 277–80).

2. Robert Minder (1902–80), French scholar of German and comparative literature, was born in Alsace to French-speaking parents at a time when Alsace-Lorraine was under German rule. During his university career he was a tireless promoter of Franco-German cultural cooperation, the historical vicissitudes of the twentieth century notwithstanding. His publications focus particularly on writers from the Rhineland. The essay referred to here is 'Heidegger und Hebel oder die Sprache von Messkirch', in *Dichter in der Gesellschaft* (Frankfurt am Main: Insel, 1966). For Heidegger's other articles on Hebel, see the Bibliography.

3. On Ernst Bloch's reception of Hebel, see the article by Johann Siebers, 'Aufenthalt im Unerhörten: Bloch's Reading of Hebel (1926–65)', in *Remembering Johann Peter Hebel: Anniversary Essays*, eds. Julian Preece and Robert Gillett, *Oxford German Studies* 40.1 (2011). This special anniversary issue of *OGS* contains a number of further interesting articles on Hebel.

4. The *Föhn* is a warm Alpine wind blowing from the south. *Wermuth* (wormwood) denotes vermouth or absinthe.

This metaphor, with the promise of a good harvest, is a reference to the tale 'Die Weizenblüte' in the *Kalender* of 1814. An equivalent English saying would be 'my ship has come in' or, to continue the botanical analogy, 'being in clover'.

5. 'Für die Fixsterne zu zählen gibt's nicht Finger genug auf der ganzen Erde' ('Die Fixsterne').

6. 'Das sah der große Kaiser Napoleon wohl ein, und im Jahr 1806, ehe er antrat die große Reise nach Jena, Berlin und Warschau, und Eylau, ließ er schreiben an die ganze Judenschaft in Frankreich, daß sie ihm sollte schicken aus ihrer Mitte verständige und gelehrte Männer aus allen Departementern des Kaisertums' ('Der Große Sanhedrin zu Paris'). Compare the standardizing translation by John Hibberd (see Hebel, *Treasure Chest*, p. 29).

7. As quoted in the German original.

8. Standard German word order places the verb at the end of a subordinate clause. Note that Sebald's own usage on occasion also deviates from this rule, particularly in longer sentences, a feature on which German critics are fond of commenting.

9. Walter Benjamin, 'A Chronicle of Germany's Unemployed: Anna Seghers' novel *Die Rettung*', trans. Edmund Jephcott, in *Selected*

Writings, vol. 4, pp. 126–33 (German text in *Gesammelte Schriften*, vol. III, pp. 530–38).

10. Probably a reference to Ernst Bloch at the end of *Das Prinzip Hoffnung*: 'etwas, das allen in die Kindheit scheint und worin noch niemand war: Heimat' (Bloch, *Werkausgabe*: vol. 5: *Das Prinzip Hoffnung* (Frankfurt am Main: Suhrkamp, 1985), p. 1628). English translation by Neville Plaice et al.: 'something which shines into the childhood of all and in which no one has yet been: homeland' (*The Principle of Hope*, vol. 3 (Oxford: Blackwell, 1986), p. 137).

11. The term *Weltfrömmigkeit* was coined by J. W. von Goethe in *Wilhelm Meister* (*Wanderjahre*, II, ch. 7).

12. Sebald omits Hebel's description 'warm' here. In Hebel's original ('Traumbilder', in *Werke*, vol. I, p. 495) the date of this dream is given as 6 November 1805.

13. The battle actually took place at Essling (on the Danube near Vienna), but no doubt Esslingen (a town on the Neckar in Württemberg) would resonate more readily with a local Alemannic readership. ('Die Kometen'.)

14. The pun in the title on *Unglück* (misery, disaster) and *Leiden*, which in German means suffering, is untranslatable here.

15. Johann Kaspar Hirzel, *Die Wirtschaft eines philosophischen Bauers* (Zurich: 1761): see Hannelore Schlaffer, ed., *Johann Peter Hebel: Schatzkästlein des Rheinischen Hausfreunds. Ein Werk in seiner Zeit* (Tübingen: Rainer Wunderlich Verlag Hermann Leins, 1980), note p. 364.

16. 'He had to chance upon a fractured society'.

17. 'Germany, awake!' 'To shake it from its lethargy, it took nothing less than the cannons of the French Emperor. This Germany which

became so terrible in the twentieth century, it is we, alas, who created it, who made it from nothing.'

18. There are variant orthographies of the Alemannic dialect in this poem, 'Die Vergänglichkeit' ('Transience'). What is reproduced in the German edition of *A Place in the Country* (the source for the present edition) differs from the edition of Hebel's work in Sebald's library: see Hebel, *Werke*, vol. 2: *Gedichte. Briefe* (Frankfurt am Main: Insel, 1968), pp. 122–6. English translation ('Transience') by Leonard Forster, in *The Penguin Book of German Verse* (Harmondsworth: Penguin Books, 1994), pp. 281–2.

J'aurais voulu que ce lac eût été l'Océan . . .

1. The Seeland (literally 'sea land' or more accurately 'lake land') is a region in Switzerland, at the foot of the Jura Mountains and bordering the cantons of Bern, Fribourg, Neuchâtel and Vaud, comprising the three lakes of Morat (Murten), Neuchâtel and Bienne (Biel) – the Lac de Bienne (or Bielersee) referred to here. It is a bilingual area on the linguistic boundary between French- and German-speaking Switzerland, and for this reason the city of Biel, Robert Walser's birthplace, is in the present translation referred to in that essay by its German name, while in the essay on Rousseau it appears in the French form, Bienne. *Seeland* is also the title of one of Walser's early collections of short prose pieces first published in 1919. Like Schattenrain (literally 'shadow ridge'), Seeland is a 'speaking name', denoting a place but also having a clear literal meaning, as well as a literary echo, within the German text.

2. In his notes to the poem 'In Alfermée' in *Across the Land and the Water*, Iain Galbraith identifies the 'exceedingly obliging host' as the critic Heinz F. Schafroth. In the September 1985 issue of *Manuskripte* (25: vol. 89/90), an article by Schafroth on Robert Walser ('Robert Walser oder die manipulierte Buchhaltung') immediately follows Sebald's article 'Das Gesetz der Schande – Macht, Messianismus und Exil in Kafkas Schloß'.

3. 'It seems to me that, in the shade of a forest, I am forgotten, free, and undisturbed, as if I no longer had any enemies' (*Rêveries of the Solitary Walker*, trans. Russell Goulbourne (Oxford: World's Classics, 2011), p. 79).

4. Hebel, 'Der Bettler' (translation by JMC).

5. 'one day this small island will astonish Europe'.

6. 'the simplest comforts of life …: linen, clothes, plates and dishes, kitchen utensils, paper, books – all these would have to be taken with me' (*Confessions*, Book XII: pp. 699–700).

7. Jean Starobinski, *Jean-Jacques Rousseau: Transparency and Obstruction*, trans. Arthur Goldhammer (Chicago and London: University of Chicago Press, 1988). Sebald quotes from the German translation by Ulrich Raulff (see Bibliography.) Goldhammer's English translation has been adapted in places (here and below) to follow Sebald's (and thus Raulff's) German more closely.

8. Sebald has *Braunwurz*, i.e. a plant from the *Scrophularia* or figwort family, possibly referring to *S. canina*, dog or French figwort, which has longer stamens than the common figwort, *S. nodosa*. The original Rousseau text has *brunelle*, i.e. *Prunella vulgaris*, or self-heal, which in German is usually known as *Brunelle*.

9. Sebald writes *Buchkapseln*, i.e. the 'seed capsules' of beech (*Buche*), in other words beechmast, although in Rousseau's French text we find *buis* (box) – which in German is *Buchs*. However, *Buch* is the German for book, and *Buchkapsel* translates as 'book box'. We may assume the German pun to be intentional.
10. Sebald's text has 'Becker'.
11. In English in the original.
12. In English in the original.

Why I grieve I do not know

1. 'Was ich traure weiß ich nicht', from Eduard Mörike, 'Verborgen-heit' ('Seclusion'), in *Mozart's Journey to Prague and a Selection of Poems*, trans. and intro. David Luke (London: Penguin Books, 2003), pp. 94–5.
2. Eduard Mörike, 'Der Feuerreiter' ('Fire Rider'), trans. Raleigh Whitinger in *Nolten the Painter* (Rochester, NY, and Woodbridge: Camden House, 2005), p. 20.
3. Wilhelm [Friedrich] Waiblinger (1804–30) was a contemporary of Mörike's at the Tübingen *Stift* (a seminary which served to prepare Protestant pastors for Württemberg), and is often referred to as 'Der wilde Waiblinger'. His poems were later collected and published by Mörike in 1844.
4. The Holy Alliance or Grand Alliance between Russia, Prussia and Austria (1815), later joined by Great Britain and (in 1818) France. It came to an end with the outbreak of the Crimean War (1853).
5. August Friedrich Ferdinand von Kotzebue (1761–1819), prolific

German dramatist. Apparently detested by nationalist liberals, he was stabbed to death by the theology student Karl Ludwig Sand, a militant member of the *Burschenschaften* or student duelling societies. The incident led to Metternich's Carlsbad Decrees, restricting academic and other freedoms.

6. Stuttgart Liederhalle: a series of concert halls in Stuttgart, first inaugurated in 1864 (Mörike was invited but could not attend, and declined in verse). Destroyed in 1943, it was replaced in 1955 by a new building and still functions as a cultural and conference centre under that name today. The present Literaturhaus Stuttgart, in an adjacent building, was inaugurated by W. G. Sebald in November 2001 (see his essay 'An Attempt at Restitution' ('Ein Versuch der Restitution') in *Campo Santo*, trans. Anthea Bell).

7. These Swabian towns in the region of Stuttgart and the surrounding area represent a chronological sketch of Mörike's rather restless life. It is no coincidence that the list ends with Fellbach; the Mörike Prize, which Sebald received there in 1997, and for which occasion this text was composed, commemorates the fact that in 1873 Mörike moved there for a while with his younger daughter, Marie, following the separation from his wife Margarethe.

8. The original alludes to the opening verse of the German national anthem (no longer sung): ['Von der Maas bis an die Memel, /] Von der Etsch bis an den Belt' (['From the Meuse to the Memel, /] From the Adige to the [Little] Belt'). In other words, from the Alps to the Baltic.

9. *Nolten the Painter*, trans. Whitinger, pp. 112–13 (translation adapted).

10. *Das Dreimäderlhaus* (The House of the Three Girls), a hugely successful 1916 Viennese operetta giving a fictionalized account of Schubert's romantic life, with music by Schubert rearranged by Heinrich Berté, and known in its English adaptation (1922) as *Lilac Time*.

11. The area of Vienna (now situated in the 9. Bezirk, Alsergrund) where Schubert was born. The name literally means 'area of the gate of Heaven', being the former site of a religious foundation (the Himmelpfortkloster, dissolved 1783).

12. Translation (from Mörike's poem 'Früh im Wagen') kindly supplied by Ray Ockenden.

13. 'Peregrina', trans. David Luke, in *Mozart's Journey to Prague and a Selection of Poems*, pp. 72–3.

14. Blautopf: Blue Pool (literally 'blue bowl') in Blaubeuren near Ulm, Swabia. In fact this episode is part of Lau's dream. For an English translation of this story, see Eduard Mörike, *Die Historie der schönen Lau / The Story of Lau, the Beautiful Water Nymph*, bilingual edition with translation by Stan Foulkes, ed. Peter Schmid (Munich: Langewiesche-Brandt, 1996). While this edition has been consulted, the translations here are JMC's own.

15. 'chess set', 'servant', 'evening round the fire spinning' (cf. sewing circle), 'spinning top', 'advantage'. The meaning of the terms seems less important here than the archaic impression conveyed.

16. *Fastnacht*, Southern German form of *Fasching*: pre-Lenten Carnival, the German equivalent of *mardi gras* / Shrove Tuesday.

Death draws nigh, time marches on

1. 'Her kommt der Tod, die Zeit geht hin', Gottfried Keller, quoted in Adolf Muschg, *Gottfried Keller* (Frankfurt am Main: Suhrkamp, 1980), p. 145.

2. *Vormärz* refers to the period before the failed March revolutions of 1848 in Germany (particularly Baden), and also to the (German-speaking) writers active then. It tends to signify a more politically engaged writing than that of the preceding Biedermeier era, usually thought of as spanning the years 1815–48.

3. Keller's second and last novel (1886) has been translated into English by Kenneth Halwas, *Martin Salander* (London: Calder, 1963).

4. Refers to Keller's story 'Kleider machen Leute' ('Clothes Make the Man') from the collection *Die Leute von Seldwyla*. For a list of English translations, see Bibliography.

5. Keller's original has *Veilchenburg* (Violet Castle).

6. *Der grüne Heinrich*; English translation by A. M. Holt, *Green Henry* (London: Calder, 1960; Oneworld Classics, 2010).

7. Full title: *The Origin of the Family, Private Property and the State*.

8. The pun on *Brockengebirge* (literally mountain of junk or bric-a-brac, but no doubt alluding to the Brocken, the highest peak in the Harz mountains, and famously the scene of the *Walpurgisnacht*, e.g. in Goethe's *Faust*) is untranslatable here.

9. Ferdinand Kürnberger (1821–79), Austrian writer who for political reasons emigrated to Germany between 1849 and 1856. The novel referred to is probably *Der Amerika-Müde. Amerikanisches Kulturbild* (The Man Who Tired of America. A Picture of American Culture) of 1855.

10. Refers to the eponymous story from the collection *Zürcher Novellen*; English translation by Paul Bernard Thomas, *The Governor of Greifensee* (NewYork: Mondial Books, 2008).

11. Used for fainting spells and cramps.

12. *Marderdreck*: formerly used as perfume. There is an old saying in German, 'to know one's musk from one's marten scat', perhaps roughly equivalent to knowing one's onions. While pine martens are rare in the UK, in continental Europe the related beech marten is a household pest, and formerly pet – cf. the (in Keller's text tame) martens in Heinrich's dream of homecoming on pp. 92–3 above.

13. Keller has *Halme[n]* ('blades of grass, grasses'), Sebald *Palmen* ('palms') – the former makes more sense, but cf. the use of palm-leaves for (somewhat absurd) decoration in Robert Walser's story from the *Bleistiftgebiet* cited above (p. 120).

14. English translation by Robert M. Browning, 'The Three Righteous Combmakers', in Gottfried Keller, *Stories*, ed. Frank Ryder (New York: Continuum, 1982) (translation adapted).

15. Cf. the eponymous chapter ('Das Meretlein') in *Der grüne Heinrich* (vol. I, ch. 5).

16. *Entschlafen* is more often used as a euphemism for dying, though it can, as here, mean falling asleep. Sebald deliberately plays on this ambiguity here.

17. Walter Benjamin, 'Gottfried Keller', in *Selected Writings*, vol. 2, trans. Rodney Livingstone (Cambridge, Mass.: Harvard University Press, 1999) (*Gesammelte Schriften*, vol. II.i, pp. 283–95).

18. Keller, 'A Village Romeo and Juliet' ('Romeo und Julia auf dem

Dorfe') from the collection *Die Leute aus Seldwyla*. Along with 'Clothes Make the Man', this is possibly the best-known of Keller's stories, and the one which has been translated the most frequently into English. The passage quoted here is adapted from the version published as *A Village Romeo and Juliet: A Tale,* intro. Edith Wharton (London: Constable, 1915 (no translator given)), p. 155. Other English translations are listed in the Bibliography.

19. 'die kolossale Kritzelei'.

Le promeneur solitaire

1. The essays by Martin Walser and Elias Canetti, along with an extract from Carl Seelig's 'walks with Robert Walser', are contained in Katharina Kerr, ed., *Über Robert Walser*, vol. 2 (Frankfurt am Main: Suhrkamp, 1978). English translations (where available) are listed in the Bibliography. The German writer Martin Walser (b. 1927) is no relation to his Swiss namesake Robert.

2. The diverse items in this list in the main reflect titles of actual texts by Walser.

3. *Das Bleistiftgebiet* is the collective term used to refer to Robert Walser's 'microscripts' or 'micrograms', written in pencil on scraps of paper in a minute, almost indecipherable script and long thought to be written in code. See pp. 128–31 above.

4. *The Robber*, trans. and intro. Susan Bernofsky (Lincoln and London: University of Nebraska Press, 2000). See also *The Tanners* (*Die Geschwister Tanner*), trans. Susan Bernofsky (New York: New Directions, 2009). The present essay first appeared as an introduc-

tion to this volume: it has been revised slightly for the present
edition. For further English translations of Walser's works, see the
Bibliography.

5. Sebald's phrase is 'ein Hellseher im Kleinen'. In Walser's introduction to his first collection, *Fritz Kochers Aufsätze* (Fritz
Kocher's Essays), the narrator explains how he has seen little of
the wider world ('die große Welt'), but 'dafür ist es ihm
vergönnt gewesen, in seiner kleinen hell zu sehen' – he has been
granted the gift of farsightedness in his own small world.
'Hellsehen' ('seeing clearly') has in German the additional
meaning of clairvoyance.

6. 'das Nachtvogelhaftscheue, in der Finsternis die Meere überflieg-
ende, in sich Hinabwimmernde'. English translation by Susan
Bernofsky (*The Robber,* p. 26).

7. *Schützenfest* ('shooting fair' or 'marksmen's festival'), a traditional
event featuring shooting competitions, food and drink stalls, and
often a funfair or circus. The *Schützenfest* is still an annual feature of
(mainly) rural life in Germany and Switzerland today.

8. Walter Benjamin, 'Robert Walser', in *Selected Writings*, vol. 2:
1927–34, trans. Rodney Livingstone (Cambridge, Mass.: Harvard
University Press, 1999) (*Gesammelte Schriften*, vol. II.i, pp. 324–8).

9. Vladimir Nabokov, *Nikolai Gogol* (London: Penguin Books, 2011).

10. Sebald uses the term *Bleikammer*, a reference to *i piombi*, the attic
cells under the roof of the Doge's palace in Venice used to house
political and other prisoners. Casanova's incarceration there is
recalled in 'All'estero' (*Vertigo*); cf. the comment there:
'presumably not a few prisoners slowly perishing beneath the
leaden roof of the palace will have been of that irrepressible species

whose desire drives them on, time after time, to the very same point' (trans. Michael Hulse), which seems equally to apply to the fate of the writer as set out here.

11. A reference to Ernst Jünger's famous novel of the Western Front in the First World War, *In Stahlgewittern* (1920). English translations (*Storm of Steel*) by Basil Creighton (1929) and Michael Hofmann (Penguin Books, 2003).

12. Heinrich von Kleist (1777–1811) wrote his first drama, *Die Familie Ghonorez* (better known as the tragedy *Die Familie Schroffenstein*) in Switzerland in 1802, where – perhaps influenced by Rousseau's views on nature – he briefly harboured hopes of settling to a rural existence. He killed himself in a suicide pact with Henriette Vogel on 21 November 1811 on the shores of the Wannsee near Berlin.

13. On Kotzebue, see 'Why I grieve I do not know' above, p. 66 and note 5, and also Walser's eponymous piece in the volume *Fritz Kochers Aufsätze. Geschichten. Aufsätze* (pp. 326–7). Otto von Kotzebue was, in fact, the son of the dramatist.

14. Vladimir Nabokov, *Speak, Memory: An Autobiography Revisited* (Harmondsworth: Penguin Books, 1987), pp. 65–6.

As Day and Night . . .

1. 'Action and passion so little separable that one no longer knows who is looking and who is being looked at, who is painting and who is being painted' (translation by Michael Hamburger, in his version of this essay in *Unrecounted*, p. 80: a closer rendering

than in the published translation of this essay listed in the Bibliography).

2. Ernst Gombrich, *Art and Illusion: A Study in the Psychology of Pictorial Representation* (London: Phaidon, 1987), p. 173.

3. Ibid.

4. Ibid., pp. 183–4.

5. In English in the original.

6. In English in the original (*Rubáiyát of Omar Khayyám*, trans. Edward FitzGerald).

Bibliography

A note on texts and translations

The Bibliography which follows lists both works referred to in W. G. Sebald's texts, and their English translations where available. An asterisk denotes an edition known to have been owned or consulted by the author. For a catalogue of Sebald's library at the time of his death, see Jo Catling/Richard Hibbitt, eds., *Saturn's Moons: W. G. Sebald – A Handbook* (Oxford: Legenda, 2011).

Where Sebald quotes directly from other writers in the text, the relevant passages are quoted, wherever possible and appropriate, from the published English translations listed below. In some cases, however, these have been adapted where necessary to fit more closely with Sebald's original. It should though also be noted that Sebald often does not quote directly, but adapts citations for his own ends.

Introduction

Arthur Lubow, 'Crossing Boundaries', in *Emergence of Memory: Conversations with W. G. Sebald,* ed. Lynne Sharon Schwartz (New York, London, etc.: Seven Stories Press, 2007), pp. 159–73

Michael Silverblatt, 'A poem of an invisible subject', in *Emergence of Memory*, pp. 77–86 (Bookworm Interview, KCRW, Santa Monica, California, 6 December 2001)

'Three Conversations with W. G. Sebald: (1) Echoes from the Past: Conversation with Piet de Moor (Brussels, 1992); (2) Lost in Translation? Conversation with Jon Cook (Norwich, 1999); (3) In This Distant Place: Conversation with Steve Wasserman (Los Angeles, 2001)', in *Saturn's Moons: W. G. Sebald – A Handbook*, eds. Jo Catling and Richard Hibbitt (Oxford: Legenda, 2011), pp. 349–75

A Comet in the Heavens

Johann Peter Hebel, *Werke*, 2 vols. (Frankfurt am Main: Insel, 1968)*

Vol. 1: *Erzählungen des Rheinischen Hausfreundes. Vermischte Schriften* ('An den Vetter: Patriotisches Mahnwort'; 'Der Brand von Moskau'; 'Die Fixsterne'; 'Der Komet von 1811'; 'Die Kometen'; 'Ein Kriegsschiff'; 'Das Unglück der Stadt Leiden'; 'Traumbilder')

Vol. 2: *Gedichte. Briefe* ('Der Bettler'; 'Die Vergänglichkeit')

Johann Peter Hebel: Schatzkästlein des Rheinischen Hausfreunds. Ein Werk in seiner Zeit, ed. Hannelore Schlaffer (Tübingen: Rainer Wunderlich Verlag Hermann Leins, 1980)*

English translations:

Johann Peter Hebel, *The Treasure Chest* (selections), intro. and trans. John Hibberd (Harmondsworth: Penguin Books, 1994) ('The Tailor at Penza' ('Der Schneider zu Pensa'); 'The Great Sanhedrin in Paris' ('Der Große Sanhedrin zu Paris'); 'The Sly Pilgrim' ('Der schlaue Pilgrim'); 'Kannitverstan' ('Kannitverstan'); 'The Emperor Napoleon and the Fruit Woman in Brienne' ('Kaiser Napoleon und die Obstfrau in Brienne'))

The Penguin Book of German Verse, trans. Leonard Forster (Harmondsworth: Penguin Books, 1994) (Hebel, 'Transience')

Secondary sources:

Walter Benjamin, *Angelus Novus: Ausgewählte Schriften*, vol. 2 (Frankfurt am Main: Suhrkamp, 1966)* ('Johann Peter Hebel'; 'Gottfried Keller')

—, *Illuminationen: Ausgewählte Schriften* (Frankfurt am Main: Suhrkamp, 1961)* ('Robert Walser')

—, 'Johann Peter Hebel (I): On the Centenary of His Death', English translation by Rodney Livingstone, in *Selected Writings 1913–1926*, vol. 1, eds. Marcus Bullock and Michael W. Jennings (Cambridge, Mass.: Belknap Press of Harvard University Press, 1996)

–, 'A Chronicle of Germany's Unemployed: Anna Segher's novel *Die Rettung*', trans. Edmund Jephcott, in *Selected Writings*, vol. 4, pp. 126–33 (*Gesammelte Schriften*, vol. III, pp. 530–38)

Ernst Bloch, *Das Prinzip Hoffnung*, 3 vols. (Frankfurt am Main: Suhrkamp, 1968)*.

–, *The Principle of Hope*, trans. Neville Plaice et al. (Oxford: Blackwell, 1986)

Jean Dutourd, *Le Feld-maréchal von Bonaparte: considérations sur les causes de la grandeur des Français et de leur décadence* (Paris: Flammarion, 1998).

Martin Heidegger, *Hebel – Der Hausfreund* (Pfullingen: Neske, 1957), reprinted in Heidegger, *Aus der Erfahrung des Denkens* (*Gesamtausgabe*, vol. 13) (Frankfurt am Main: Klostermann, 1983); English translation by Bruce V. Foltz and Michael Heim as 'Hebel – Friend of the House', in *Contemporary German Philosophy* 3 (1983)

Other works on Hebel by Heidegger are as follows:

–, 'Die Sprache Johann Peter Hebels' (1955), in Martin Heidegger, *Aus der Erfahrung des Denkens*

–, *Gespräch mit Hebel. Rede beim Schatzkästlein zum Hebeltag 1956* (Lörrach: Hebelbund, n.d.). (= *Aus der Schriftenreihe des Hebelbundes Sitz Lörrach e.V.*, Nr. 4), reprinted in Hanns Uhl (ed.), *Hebeldank. Bekenntnis zum alemannischen Geist in sieben Reden beim Schatzkästlein* (Freiburg: Rombach, 1964)

–, 'Dank bei der Verleihung des staatlichen Hebelgedenkpreises', in *Hebel-Feier. Reden zum 200. Geburtstag* (Karlsruhe: Müller, 1960), reprinted in *Hebel in Ehren. 50 Jahre Hebel-Preis* (Bühl-Moos: Elster, 1986) (= *Allmende*, Nr. 13)

Robert Minder, 'Heidegger und Hebel oder die Sprache von Messkirch', in *Dichter in der Gesellschaft: Erfahrungen mit deutscher und französischer Literatur* (Frankfurt am Main: Insel, 1966);* also includes 'Johann Peter Hebel und die französische Heimatliteratur'

Remembering Johann Peter Hebel: Anniversary Essays, eds. Julian Preece and Robert Gillett, *Oxford German Studies* 40.1 (2011)

J'aurais voulu que ce lac eût été l'Océan . . .

Jean-Jacques Rousseau, *Les Confessions*, 2 vols. (Paris: Gallimard, 1980)*

—, *La Nouvelle Héloise*, 6 vols. (Paris: Librairie des Bibliophiles, 1889)*

—, *Träumereien eines einsamen Spaziergängers: Der fünfte Spaziergang*, trans. Franz Bäschlin (Biel: Verkehrsverein Biel und Umgebung (Schweiz), n.d.)* (*Les rêveries du promeneur solitaire*: Cinquième promenade)

English translations:

Jean-Jacques Rousseau, *Confessions* (trans. anon.), ed. and intro. P. N. Furbank (London: Everyman's Library, repr. 1992)

—, *Meditations of a Solitary Walker*, trans. Peter France (Harmondsworth: Penguin 60s Classics, 1995)*

—, *Reveries of the Solitary Walker,* trans. Peter France (Harmondsworth: Penguin Classics, 1979) (Jean-Jacques Rousseau, *Les Rêveries du promeneur solitaire*)

—, *Reveries of the Solitary Walker*, trans. Russell Goldbourne (Oxford: World's Classics, 2011)

Secondary sources:

Werner Henzi, *St Petersinsel und J-J Rousseau's Aufenthalt 1765* (Biel, 1956)*

Jean Starobinski, *Jean-Jacques Rousseau: la transparence et l'obstacle: suivi de sept essais sur Rousseau.* (Paris: Gallimard, 1971; English translation Arthur Goldhammer, *Jean-Jacques Rousseau: Transparency and Obstruction* (Chicago and London: University of Chicago Press, 1988)

—, *Rousseau: Eine Welt von Widerständen*, German trans. Ulrich Raulff (Frankfurt am Main: Fischer Taschenbuch, 1993)*

Why I grieve I do not know

Eduard Mörike, *Sämtliche Werke* (Munich: Hanser, 1964)*
(Prose: *Das Stuttgarter Hutzelmännlein*, including *Historie der schönen Lau: Maler Nolten.* Poems: 'Verborgenheit'; 'Der Feuerreiter'; 'Früh im Wagen'; 'Peregrina')

English translations:

Eduard Mörike, *Mozart's Journey to Prague and a Selection of Poems*, trans. and intro. David Luke (London: Penguin Classics, 2003) ('Peregrina'; 'Seclusion' ('Verborgenheit'))

—, *Die Historie der schönen Lau / The Story of Lau, the Beautiful Water Nymph*, bilingual edition with translation by Stan Foulkes, ed. Peter Schmid (Munich: Langewiesche-Brandt, 1996)

—, *Nolten the Painter*, trans. Raleigh Whitinger (Rochester, NY, and Woodbridge: Camden House, 2005) (*Maler Nolten*; includes the poem 'Fire Rider' ('Der Feuerreiter'))

Secondary sources:

Hans Egon Holthusen, *Eduard Mörike in Selbstzeugnissen und Bilddokumenten* (Reinbek bei Hamburg: Rowohlt Bildmonographie, 1976)*

Birgit Mayer, *Eduard Mörike* (Stuttgart: Metzler, 1987)*

Death draws nigh, time marches on

Gottfried Keller, *Werke*, 4 vols. (Leipzig: Insel, 1921)*
   Vol. 1: *Gedichte; Das Sinngedicht;* Vol. 2: *Der grüne Heinrich;* Vol. 3: *Die Leute von Seldwyla; Sieben Legenden; Erzählungen;* Vol. 4: *Zürcher Novellen; Martin Salander; Therese*

—, *Der grüne Heinrich*, 4 vols. (Stuttgart and Berlin: Cotta, 1919)*

English translations:

Gottfried Keller, *Green Henry*, trans. A. M. Holt (London: Calder, 1960; Oneworld Classics, 2010) (*Der grüne Heinrich*)

—, *Martin Salander*, trans. Kenneth Halwas (London: Calder, 1963)

—, *The Governor of Greifensee*, trans. Paul Bernard Thomas (New York: Mondial Books, 2008) ('Der Landvogt von Greifensee', from *Zürcher Novellen*)

—, *A Village Romeo and Juliet: A Tale,* intro. Edith Wharton (London: Constable, 1915 (no translator given))

—, *Stories*, ed. Frank G. Ryder (New York: Continuum, 1982) ('Clothes Make the Man', trans. Harry Steinhauer ('Kleider machen Leute'); 'The Three Righteous Combmakers', trans. Robert M. Browning ('Die drei gerechten Kammacher'); 'A Village Romeo and Juliet', trans. Paul Bernard Thomas (adapted Kenneth Ryder) ('Romeo und Julia auf dem Dorfe') all from *Die Leute von Seldwyla*)

Further translations:

'Clothes Make the Man', trans. Michael Fleming, in *Eight German Novellas*, ed. Andrew J. Webber (Oxford: World Classics, 1997)

'A Village Romeo and Juliet', trans. Robert Taylor, in *Three German Stories* (London: Calder and Boyars, 1966)

Secondary sources:

Jakob Baechtold, *Gottfried Kellers Leben*, 3 vols. (Stuttgart and Berlin: Cotta, 1895–1903)*

Walter Benjamin, 'Gottfried Keller', in *Selected Writings*, vol. 2, trans. Rodney Livingstone (Cambridge, Mass.: Harvard University Press, 1999)

Adolf Muschg, *Gottfried Keller* (Frankfurt am Main: Suhrkamp, 1980)*

Wolfgang Schlüter, *Walter Benjamin: Der Sammler und das geschlossene Kästchen* (Darmstadt: Jürgen Hüsser, 1993)*

Le promeneur solitaire

Robert Walser, *Romane und Erzählungen*, 6 vols. (Frankfurt am Main: Suhrkamp, 1984)*

Vol. 1: *Geschwister Tanner*; Vol. 2: *Der Gehülfe*; Vol. 3: *Jakob von Gunten*; Vol. 4: *Der Räuber*; Vol. 5: *Erzählungen 1907–1916*; Vol. 6: *Erzählungen 1917–1932*

—, *Fritz Kochers Aufsätze. Geschichten. Aufsätze* (*Das Gesamtwerk*, vol. I) (Geneva, Hamburg: Kossodo, 1972)* ('Ballonfahrt'; 'Einleitung'; 'Fritz Kocher: Stumme Minuten'; 'Kotzebue'; 'Kleist in Thun'; 'Simon')

—, *Poetenleben. Seeland. Die Rose* (*Das Gesamtwerk*, vol. III) (Geneva, Hamburg: Kossodo, 1967)* ('Widmann')

—, *Phantasieren: Prosa aus der Berliner und Bieler Zeit* (*Das Gesamtwerk*, vol. VI) (Geneva, Hamburg: Kossodo, 1966)* ('Abschied'; 'Am See'; 'Asche, Nadel, Bleistift und Zündhölzchen'; 'Sonntag'; 'Die Untergasse')

—, *Festzug. Prosa aus der Bieler und Berner Zeit* (*Das Gesamtwerk*, vol. VII) (Geneva, Hamburg: Kossodo, 1966) ('München')

—, *Aus dem Bleistiftgebiet. Mikrogramme aus den Jahren 1924–1925.* vol. 1: *Prosa* (Frankfurt am Main, Suhrkamp, 1985)*

('Leihet mir zum Anhören einer der vorsichtigsten Geschichten
...'; 'Und nun spielte er leider Klavier ...')
—, Aus dem Bleistiftgebiet, vol. 3: 'Räuber'-Roman; 'Felix'-Szenen
(Frankfurt am Main, Suhrkamp, 1986)*

English translations:

Robert Walser, The Assistant, trans. Susan Bernofsky (London:
Penguin Books, 2008)
—, Jakob von Gunten, trans. Christopher Middleton (Austin and
London: University of Texas Press, 1969; New York: New York
Review Books, 1999); also under the title of Institute Benjamenta
(London: Serpent's Tail, 1995)
—, The Robber, trans. and intro. Susan Bernofsky (Lincoln, Nebr.,
and London: University of Nebraska Press, 2000)
—, The Tanners, trans. Susan Bernofsky (New York: New Direc-
tions, 2009)
—, Masquerade and Other Stories, trans. Susan Bernofsky (Baltimore
and London: Johns Hopkins University Press, 1990) ('Simon')
—, Selected Stories, trans. Christopher Middleton and others, intro.
Susan Sontag (Manchester: Carcanet, 1982; reissued New
York: New York Review Books, 2002) ('Balloon Journey'
('Ballonfahrt'); 'Kleist in Thun')
—, Speaking to the Rose: Writings 1912–1932, trans. Christopher
Middleton (Lincoln, Nebr., and London: University of
Nebraska Press, 2005) ('Brentano'; 'The Back Alley' ('Die
Untergasse'); 'And now he was playing, alas, the piano ('Und nun
spielte er leider Klavier'))

Robert Walser Rediscovered: Stories, Fairy-Tale Plays, and Critical Responses, ed. Mark Harman (Hanover, NH, and London: University Press of New England for Dartmouth College, 1985); also includes: Walter Benjamin, 'Robert Walser', trans. Mark Harman; Elias Canetti, 'Robert Walser', trans. Joachim Neugroschel

The Review of Contemporary Fiction: Robert Walser Number, eds. Susan Bernofsky and Tom Whalen, *The Review of Contemporary Fiction* 12.1 (Spring 1992); also includes: Martin Walser, 'A Poet Apart: On Robert Walser', trans. Susan Bernofsky and Tom Whalen

Further recent translations:

Berlin Stories, trans. Susan Bernofsky (New York: New York Review Books, 2012)

Microscripts, trans. Susan Bernofsky (New York: New Directions, 2010)

Oppressive Light. Selected Poems by Robert Walser, trans. and ed. Daniele Pantano (Pittsburgh, PA: Black Lawrence Press, 2012)

Secondary sources:

Walter Benjamin, 'Robert Walser', in *Selected Writings*, vol. 2: *1927–34*, trans. Rodney Livingstone (Cambridge, Mass.: Harvard University Press, 1999) (and see above)

Robert Mächler, *Das Leben Robert Walsers* (Geneva, Hamburg: Kossodo, 1966)*

Über Robert Walser (vol. 2), ed. Katharina Kerr (Frankfurt am Main: Suhrkamp, 1978);* includes Elias Canetti, 'Einige Aufzeichnungen zu Robert Walser' (1973); Martin Walser,

'Alleinstehender Dichter. Über Robert Walser' (1963); Carl
   Seelig, '27. Juli 1943. Eine Wanderung mit Robert Walser'
   (1957)
Vladimir Nabokov, *Nikolaj Gogol*, German trans. Jochen
   Neuburger (1990) (*Gesammelte Werke*, ed. Dieter E. Zimmer,
   vol. 16)*
—, *Erinnerung, sprich*, German trans. Dieter E. Zimmer et al.
   (1991) (*Gesammelte Werke*, vol. 22)* (*Speak, Memory*)
—, *Speak, Memory: An Autobiography Revisited* (Harmondsworth:
   Penguin Books, 1987)*
—, *Nikolai Gogol* (London: Penguin Books, 2011)

As Day and Night . . .

Jan Peter Tripp, *Die Aufzählung der Schwierigkeiten: Arbeiten von
   1985–92* (Offenburg: Reiff Schwarzwaldverlag, 1993)*
Edward Fitzgerald, trans., *Rubáiyát of Omar Khayyám*, ed. and
   intro. Dick Davis (Harmondsworth: Penguin Books, 1989)*
E. H. Gombrich, *Art and Illusion: A Study in the Psychology of Pictorial
   Representation* (London: Phaidon, 1983)
Maurice Merleau-Ponty, *L'Oeil et l'Esprit*, ed. Claude Lefort (Paris:
   Gallimard, 2001), 'Eye and Mind', trans. Michael B. Smith, in *The
   Merleau-Ponty Aesthetics Reader: Philosophy and Painting*, ed. Galen
   A. Johnson (Evanston, IU: Northwestern University Press, 1993)

Acknowledgements

Just as it was an honour and a pleasure to share the teaching of German literature at UEA with Max Sebald at the time he was writing these essays, so too it has been a privilege, and a pleasure, to translate them into English. I am very grateful to the Estate of W. G. Sebald and the Wylie Agency; the Deutsches Literatur-archiv Marbach; the Europäisches Übersetzer-Kollegium Straelen, and the DAAD for their generous assistance and support. Among the many individuals who have generously shared their advice and insights, particular thanks are due to: Gertrud Aebischer-Sebald, Anthea Bell, Susan Bernofsky, Patrick Charbonneau, Iain Galbraith, Heide Gerland, Russell Goulbourne, Mark Handsley, Ria van Hengel, Richard Hibbitt, Luke Ingram, Anna Kelly, Scott Moyers, Ray Ockenden, Brigid Purcell, Clive Scott, Ada Vigliani and Anthony Vivis, for all their assistance, comments and suggestions.